Peter Ward

THE ADVENTURES OF CHARLES DARWIN

Illustrated by
Annabel Large

Cambridge University Press

Cambridge

London   New York   New Rochelle
Melbourne   Sydney

CAMBRIDGE UNIVERSITY PRESS
Cambridge, New York, Melbourne, Madrid, Cape Town, Singapore, São Paulo, Delhi

Cambridge University Press
The Edinburgh Building, Cambridge CB2 8RU, UK

Published in the United States of America by Cambridge University Press, New York

www.cambridge.org
Information on this title: www.cambridge.org/9780521310741

First published 1982
Paperback edition first published 1986
Re-issued in this digitally printed version 2009

A catalogue record for this publication is available from the British Library

Library of Congress Catalogue Card Number: 81–21751

ISBN 978-0-521-24510-4 hardback
ISBN 978-0-521-31074-1 paperback

The author and publisher gratefully acknowledge
the help of Down House and the Royal College
of Surgeons of England

For Philippa, Sarah and Rebecca

Contents

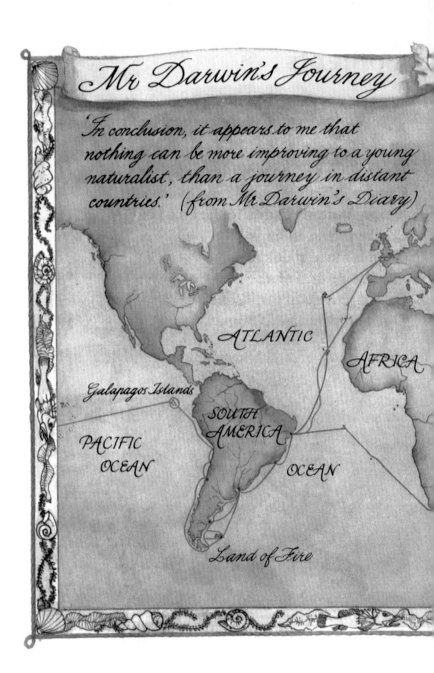

Mr Darwin's Journey

'In conclusion, it appears to me that nothing can be more improving to a young naturalist, than a journey in distant countries.' (from Mr Darwin's Diary)

ATLANTIC

AFRICA

Galapagos Islands

SOUTH AMERICA

PACIFIC OCEAN

OCEAN

Land of Fire

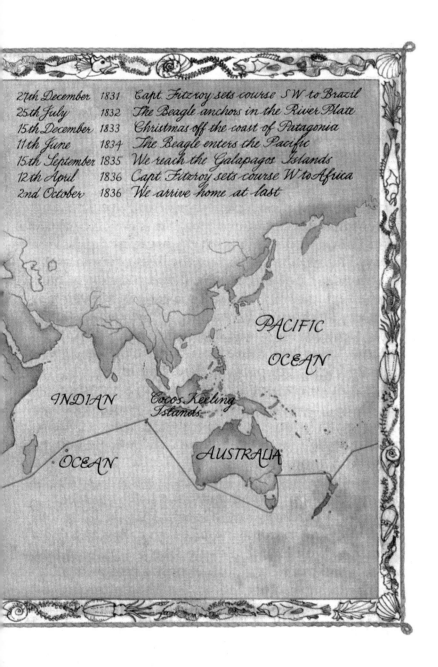

27th December	1831	Capt. Fitzroy sets course SW to Brazil
25th July	1832	The Beagle anchors in the River Plate
15th December	1833	Christmas off the coast of Patagonia
11th June	1834	The Beagle enters the Pacific
15th September	1835	We reach the Galapagos Islands
12th April	1836	Capt. Fitzroy sets course W to Africa
2nd October	1836	We arrive home at last

PACIFIC

OCEAN

INDIAN   Cocos Keeling
Islands

OCEAN   AUSTRALIA

5

The Beetle Man

My name is George Carter. You will never have heard of me. To be honest I am no-one special, yet I know of tales to make a person's hair stand on end. In my time I have kept company with famous men. I have sailed the Seven Seas and have been to faraway places. Three times have I been shipwrecked and thought that my last hour had come. In the face of the storm I have seen grown men cry, weep and plead for mercy. The seas have claimed the lives of some of my best friends. Life has been hard and rough, yet I am not the sort to settle. The salt sea runs in my veins as befits any lad born in Plymouth.

The story I want to tell begins in the year 1831. At the time, I was little more than a boy. Our family was separated after my parents died of a fever. My two elder sisters were sent away to work in a grand house and I was not to see them again. I, young George, was taken in by an uncle. In his way, he was good to me, but he had no real liking for children. He had, as they say, 'naval connections'. Uncle John had a brother in the Navy and through him it was arranged that I would join the company of a sailing vessel.

'You're a big boy now, George,' Uncle John told me. 'I'm going to make a man of you. You're to be a cabin boy upon H.M.S. Beagle. She is a ten-gun brig and sets sail from Plymouth in only a few weeks!'

My heart sank. Now I admit that I had often dreamt of going to sea, yet I did not think it would happen like this.

'You'll be going on a long journey, young George. The Beagle sails for South America. Why, I've heard

6

that she may sail round the world. Perhaps you'll make your fortune!'.

I tried to smile, out of politeness, but what could I say? My uncle meant well.

I wept as I bade him goodbye and I thought of my sisters in the grand house and wondered what they were doing. That was on Christmas Day, 1831. It was the most miserable Christmas I have ever spent. The Beagle set sail two days later and, as we headed towards the open sea, I looked back on Plymouth harbour with great sadness.

Our ship tossed like a cork upon the sea. I lay sea-sick and ill upon the open wooden deck and was soaked through. The sailors were not a bad lot, but a sailing ship is no place for slacking. They spent their time gathering in the sails and making repairs but, when they got the chance, they took time off to tease me dreadfully.

The officers were a proud bunch and kept very much to themselves. It was one of my jobs to sweep their cabins. My most important job was to see to the cabin of the Captain. Of Captain FitzRoy I shall have much to say.

In the beginning, there was just one person who showed me kindness. This was a man not like the rest of the crew and I remember the first time he spoke to me. It was not long after we had set sail and I had gone down to the Captain's cabin. I was a little afraid because Captain FitzRoy was known to have a fierce temper. Timidly, I knocked at his door.

'Enter!' called a voice, not unfriendly.

I opened the door and stood just inside the room. A tall young man got up from his chair at the table. He smiled.

'Come in! Come in! Why, you're nearly shaking!

No-one's going to eat you! What's your name, boy?

'George, sir,' I stammered, 'George Carter.'

The young man held out a hand and shook mine warmly and firmly.

'Darwin,' he said, 'Charles Darwin. Pleased to meet you, young George. Come in and sit down.'

He offered me a seat and was most courteous. I think he knew I was not happy and invited me to share my troubles with him. As I told him of my unhappiness I glanced around the room. At that time I was not to know that I would spend much of the voyage there. I was fascinated. Mr Darwin had a pile of books on the table and he had been unpacking a box of glass jars. He had a microscope, too. Also on the table, stacked one on top of the other, were some small boxes. I could not resist asking what he was doing.

'You may well ask, George,' he said. 'The Captain gets cross with me as really this is his cabin. I share it with him but he says I take up all the room!'

I asked him what he kept in his little boxes. I thought it might be tobacco.

'No, George, not tobacco! Nor money, nor jewels. Something far more precious!'

I could not imagine what he meant.

'See!' he cried. 'Let me show you!' He opened one of the boxes and I drew back in horror.

'Precious?' I exclaimed. 'They're cockroaches! Disgusting!'

Mr Darwin laughed. 'These are not cockroaches. They're beetles – very similar to cockroaches, I'll grant you. I collected these in England, last summer but, as yet, I have not had time to examine them properly. I shall include them in my collection.'

I gave him a questioning look. 'Mr Darwin, I've

never heard of anyone keeping dead beatles before. Why do you do it?'

This seemed to shock him a little. 'I've always collected beetles,' he replied, 'and spiders, dragon-flies and butterflies. I have some fine collections at home. Perhaps you think that strange, but then, most people do. You see I am a naturalist.'

'A naturalist?' I asked him. 'I've never heard of that. What does a naturalist do, sir?'

He showed great interest in my question.

'Well, George,' said Mr Darwin, 'it's hard to know where to begin. I study plants and animals, and I make collections of them. Why, I even have a collection of rocks and fossils.'

This I could not understand. It seemed to me a very strange pastime. What could you do with a lot of life-less rocks?

'I hope you will not think me rude, Mr Darwin. If you are so keen on collecting things from the country-side, I do not see why you have come aboard the Beagle. You will find no butterflies on board ship!'

He raised his eyebrows and smiled. 'I am the ship's

naturalist,' he explained. 'Captain FitzRoy invited me to join him on his expedition. I have always wanted to travel, and now we're sailing for the Tropics where we shall see wonderful new lands. I hope to discover new animals and I want to look at the rocks we may come across. However, I need to get organised before we sight land. I am just sorting out my things. Perhaps it will be possible for you to help me sometimes.'

Mr Darwin seemed to be a clever gentleman and I could see no way in which I could help him.

'Mr Darwin, I shall be of no use to you. You have been educated, I can tell that. Why, sir, I have never even attended school.'

'School?' he questioned. 'School? Don't talk to me about school. Little I learnt there, I can tell you! The happiest day of my life so far, George, was the day I left school! Why, they stopped me doing all the things I wanted to do. There was no nature study. After my mother died, when I was only nine years old, father sent me to Dr Butler's school in Shrewsbury.'

I had never been to Shrewsbury. To be honest, I had never seen any town other than Plymouth.

'No George, school did me little good, I believe. Dr Butler didn't teach us to think for ourselves. He had a very poor opinion of me. Some of the boys had a strange view of me, too. They used to call me Gas!'

'Gas?' I asked him. 'Why did they call you that?'

'It was my brother's fault,' he replied. 'Brother Erasmus was interested in science. We used to mess around with chemicals in the toolshed at the bottom of the garden! It was rather a dangerous thing to do, I suppose. It's a wonder we did not blow each other up.'

10

Mr Darwin asked me to help him unpack yet another assortment of boxes. While we did this he continued to tell me about his earlier life.

'I was bored at school. Father was disappointed in me and at the age of sixteen I was taken away and sent to Edinburgh.'

'Edinburgh?' I asked him. 'Please, Mr Darwin, where's that?'

This drew another smile from him. 'Edinburgh is the capital of Scotland,' he explained. 'Father wanted me to become a doctor. He has been a doctor for much of his life and I suppose he wanted his son to follow him!'

I blinked with astonishment. What was Mr Darwin? He was a naturalist and a sailor. Now he was telling me he was a doctor!

'Should I call you Doctor Darwin, sir?'

He laughed out loud. 'Failed Dr Darwin, you can call me, George! No! I never sat my examinations. Doctoring was not for me. So off I went to Cambridge!'

Now I was truly confused. Mr Darwin did seem to be a bit of a traveller.

'Father decided that I should become a clergyman. He wanted me to be a vicar, I suppose, and preach fine sermons.'

Now I began to wonder if Mr Darwin was teasing me. Naturalist, scientist, doctor, clergyman! What was he going to say next? Tinker! Tailor! perhaps?

'I failed, of course!' he laughed. 'I did pass some of my examinations, but I never became a clergyman. I had other things to do at Cambridge!'

'Mr Darwin,' I said to him. 'Have you decided, now, what you want to do?'

'Yes!' he said, 'I know exactly what I want to do and

11

what I want to become.'

'What's that?' I asked him.

'Why, isn't it obvious?' he cried. 'A naturalist, of course. That's what I've always wanted to be. You shall help me, George. We shall learn things together!'

Mr Darwin went on to tell me of his time at Cambridge. He spoke of clever men called professors. One was called Adam Sedgwick, who studied the rocks of the earth. He was especially interested in volcanoes and earthquakes. Mr Darwin and Professor Sedgwick used to go on long walks and collect rocks and fossils. No wonder Mr Darwin never had time to study to become a clergyman.

'There was another professor, who helped me,' he said. 'He was John Stevens Henslow, and he was Professor of Botany.'

Here was another new word for me. Botany – I had

no idea of what it meant.

'Botany,' Mr Darwin told me 'is the study of plants – trees, flowers mosses, ferns – you know the sort of thing. Professor Henslow is the man who gave me the idea of joining the Beagle as the ship's naturalist. It was he who knew that Captain FitzRoy was willing to share his cabin. Even so, at one time it was not certain that I would be allowed to join the expedition.'

I could not help but wonder at what he meant by that.

'You see, George, my father is a very disappointed man because he thinks I have let him down. He says I am unable to get down to hard work. He didn't want me to come on this voyage. It was my uncle who persuaded him to see sense, my Uncle Josiah.'

'Your uncle?' I cried. 'So your uncle was the person who helped you join the Navy! We have something in common, Mr Darwin, for it was my uncle who got

13

me on the Beagle, too! Not that I was very willing, mind you!'

Mr Darwin smiled and nodded. 'True,' he said. 'However, I very nearly did not come at all. You see, I had to meet Captain FitzRoy first. I travelled by coach to London to see him. He was very polite, of course, a true gentleman. Yet I felt there was something about me that he did not, at first, like!'

For me, it was impossible to imagine anything about Mr Darwin that a person could not like. Was there another side to his character? Was there a dark mystery about him? What could it be that Captain FitzRoy had failed to like?

'My nose!' chortled Mr Darwin. 'The shape of my nose!'

I began to laugh.

'Captain FitzRoy has the idea that you can tell a person's character by the shape of his face. Apparently, I had the wrong kind of nose for him! He told someone that a person with my sort of nose would lack energy and determination. It was not the sort of nose that would face up to the hardships of a lengthy naval cruise!'

He put his finger to his lips. I was forbidden to laugh any longer as the Captain might have walked into the cabin at any moment. Somehow, Captain FitzRoy got over the problem of Mr Darwin's nose. He changed his opinion of Mr Darwin for no person I have met before or since has ever possessed his drive and energy. Yet I am sorry to tell you that Mr Darwin and the Captain had some fine old arguments. However, that is for later. For now, it is time to introduce you to the little ship that was to be our home for the next five years. The Royal Navy's sailing brig, H.M.S. Beagle.

A ducking for Mr Darwin

H.M.S. Beagle was a warship, and she could fight her way out of trouble. More than once were we fired upon. Some of the sailors were old hands, others were still learning their trade. Yet none was as new to it as I was. It never ceased to excite me the way they swarmed up the rigging. The coxswain had a shrill pipe and at his command the agile sailors climbed to the tops of the yardarms. These were the great cross-pieces attached to the high masts. They carried enormous sails neatly tucked up along their length. 'Man the yards!' was the order given on the pipe to take in or to let out the sails. It was tricky and danger-ous work and this was particularly so in heavy seas or driving squalls of rain. The sailors told me of fearful accidents which had befallen their comrades on other voyages.

Down below, which means below the deck, were the stores. In the hold where food was stored, there was not an inch of wasted space. I was told that hun-dreds of barrels of salted meat had been taken on board, and I have no idea of the number of bags of flour which were stored there. There were dried ship's biscuits and, if you were lucky, you could sneak a handful of raisins. Most important of all was the fresh water we took on board. This came in large wooden barrels called casks. All this was as new to Mr Darwin as it was to me.

He told me how, on the first night on board, he had problems getting into his hammock.

'I felt such a fool, George! First, I tried jumping into it, and found myself rolling out on the other side! Then I picked myself up and decided to ride it like a

15

horse. I gripped the thing by the neck and then threw my legs over it. It reared and bucked sideways. The harder I tried the farther I pushed it away from me. Why, I nearly broke my neck!'

Poor Mr Darwin! It was I who told him of the correct method of sleeping in a hammock. I had learnt it from the sailors.

'Sit in it first, sir, right in the middle, with your legs dangling over the side. Then twist sideways, throw your head back and bring your feet up. It's simple!' It struck me that I had taught Mr Darwin something!

Our next lesson, however, was a sharper one. I have already told you that Christmas 1831 was the most miserable of my life. Yet in some ways I was lucky. The crew had been allowed off the ship for Christmas Day itself. The very next day, Boxing Day, dawned clear and bright. There was a calm sea and we could have set sail at the start of our voyage. Yet if we had done so, we would have gone without half the crew! Many of them defied Captain FitzRoy's orders and did not return to the ship. They had got themselves horribly drunk over Christmas and were in no mood for sailoring. When they finally drifted back they were severely spoken to by the officers. Some of the sailors became very rude to the officers and, because of this, spent the rest of Boxing Day locked up in heavy chains.

Two days later, I noticed that Mr Darwin was very quiet and extremely upset. A number of the sailors were flogged at the mast for their bad behaviour. It was the flogging which had upset Mr Darwin. It is a terrible punishment. Their backs bore the marks of the lash and blood ran from their wounds. Discipline on the Beagle was very harsh.

Only two days after setting sail we had travelled

over four hundred miles. This meant that we soon reached the Bay of Biscay. Mr Darwin lay in his cabin most of the time and was dreadfully seasick.

He groaned, 'Do you know, George, I have never felt more ill in my whole life? I cannot think why I ever wanted to come on such a voyage. Seasickness is beyond description. I feel so wretched!'

I noted how poor Mr Darwin kept a diary of everything that happened to him. He wrote it even in his very worst moments.

I was more fortunate than Mr Darwin. Although I was quite seasick at the start of the voyage, I gradually grew used to the rolling of the ship. I was, therefore, able to help him in his worst moments. Yet even he enjoyed the parts of the voyage when a fair wind pushed us along and the Beagle carved through the waves at some speed. I realised that Captain FitzRoy was an excellent sailor and this was something for which I was always thankful. A sailing ship with a poor captain is a dangerous place to be!

About six weeks after we had set out, it would have been the middle of February, a strange incident took place. We had been sailing through tropical waters and Mr Darwin warned me that something unusual was going to happen.

'George, we are about to cross the Equator. We shall sail from the northern half of the world into the southern half. Sailors have weird customs and I fear that we shall suffer some of them. We are about to be shaved!'

Shaved? I was hardly old enough to shave! What could Mr Darwin mean?

'You and I are griffins, George. That's the sailor's expression for those who are new to the sea and have not yet crossed the Equator. They hold a ceremony especially for us. We are shaved and ducked in water, I believe. It is all done in good fun, so they say, and there is no wriggling out of it.'

No sooner had he spoken than we were attacked. Four rough sailors grabbed us and pushed us down below deck. Before we could recover our senses, they battened down the hatches. It was terribly dark but as our eyes got used to it we realised that we were not alone. In fact, there were another thirty sailors down there with us! They were young and, like ourselves, had never crossed the Equator. It was hot and stuffy in our temporary prison and we longed for fresh air.

Suddenly, a hatch was opened and four older sailors climbed down the ladder. They informed us that they were Neptune's constables. Neptune was said to be the great King who ruled all the oceans. I hid in a dark corner and, to my shame, saw that it was Mr Darwin they had come for first. He was dragged up the ladder and out onto the deck. The hatch was battened down again, and the young sailors and I listened, terrified, in the gloom. What could they be doing to him? We heard cheers and shouts and great splashings of water.

It was not long before the hatch was re-opened, and Neptune's constables clambered down to fetch another unfortunate victim. As quick as a flash I leapt up the ladder and scurried on hands and knees to the bow of the ship. There I hid in a locker sometimes used to store canvas. I lay in terror for most of the day. When things died down and the sailors had gone back to their normal duties, I slid out of my hiding place. That night, I plucked up courage and crept down to Mr Darwin's cabin where I found him writing by the light of an oil lamp. He glanced up when I opened the door, and his face looked battered and raw.

'Forgive me, Mr Darwin,' I pleaded in a soft voice. 'I was such a coward. I greatly feared what they would do to me. You see, I cannot swim, sir, and I was terrified that they would throw me overboard!'

Mr Darwin smiled. It was a kind smile of understanding. 'You are a very sensible boy, George,' he told me. 'I wish I had your wits. Yet what they did to us was in good humour, and no-one was thrown overboard!'

I felt some relief at this and asked him to tell me what the sailors had done to him.

'It is part of their ceremony, George, as I told you. I was a griffin and had never crossed the Equator. When I was captured below deck I was blindfolded. Then I was dragged up the ladder and let out. First, I was deluged with water! Buckets and buckets of the stuff! Soaked right through. That was only the beginning!'

My eyes must have grown round in wonder. What happened next, I asked him?

'They sat me on a wooden plank. My blindfold was removed and my face plastered with shaving cream.'

Now, I happened to remember that Mr Darwin had already shaved that particular morning. I had been tidying the cabin as he had done so. I did not understand.

'Not real shaving cream, George, but a vile mixture of pitch, which is a black, sticky sort of tar, and paint. This was worked roughly into my chin and scraped off with a razor. It was not a proper razon but an old iron hoop which I expect they keep specially for the ceremony. It was rusty! At a given signal, the plank

19

was tilted and the next thing I knew was that I was thrown into the air, head over heels!'

I could hardly believe my ears. I thought that the sailors must have gone crazy and asked if Captain FitzRoy knew of these goings on.

'Captain FitzRoy,' Mr Darwin told me, 'was the chief actor! He enjoyed it as much as the rest. Of course it must have happened to him on his first voyage across the equator. Not many escape the ordeal, George!'

Here, I winced a little. I did feel something of a coward, I confess.

'Then, George,' Mr Darwin went on, 'I landed in a great tub of water. Two sailors gave me a ducking and all but drowned me. A great cheer went up from the onlookers, and I was through my part of the cere-

mony. King Neptune had been satisfied. Now, I have to be patient and wait for my poor face to recover. I have managed to rub off the worst of the muck!'

Poor Mr Darwin! No wonder his face was red and raw. He told me that the sailors who followed him received far worse treatment.

It made me wonder what was the true purpose of our voyage. I had little idea of where we were sailing. We had already reached two island ports, although at one we did not stop. Mr Darwin told me that the Beagle was a very important ship. We were to sail to South America and later we would voyage across the Pacific Ocean.

'You see, George,' he explained, 'Captain FitzRoy has much work to do. It is his job to sail along the coasts of certain foreign lands and make all sorts of

measurements. This will help the Navy to draw good accurate maps of the coastlines. Also, as we sail, we shall measure the depth of the water. One day, as a result of this voyage, charts will be drawn up. They will then be printed and used by other ships. If our measurements are correct, these ships will sail more safely. There is a great deal to do. The Beagle will sail right round the world and we shall not return to England for some years!'

Right round the world! So Uncle John was right. What would my dear sisters be doing in all that time? Would I ever see them again and, if so, would they recognise their brother George?

With questions such as these turning over in my mind, I crept back to my hammock. I felt much relieved that no-one seemed to have realised that I had escaped King Neptune's ceremony. As I lay in my hammock I could not sleep. Many thoughts crossed my mind. Could it be that I would be the youngest boy ever to sail right round the world? After all, not many ships had made such journeys. I wondered if Sir Francis Drake had taken a cabin boy of my age on board The Golden Hind when he first sailed round the world. That night, I dreamt of pirates and buccaneers, and tropical islands and King Neptune.

Grasshoppers, lizards and kingfishers

A few days later I was awoken by my shipmates who were in a state of great excitement.

'Quickly, young George,' said the coxswain, 'get dressed and get down to the Captain's cabin. Your friend Mr Darwin has gone completely mad. He's wandering round talking about dust and shouting the word at the top of his voice. We'll have to lock him in the hold if he carries on like this.'

I was very distressed to hear this news and I leapt from my hammock and sped towards the Captain's cabin, hurriedly pulling on my shirt and tripping over my untied shoelaces as I staggered along the narrow passageways.

'George! It's a wonderful day! Such excitement – why it's enough to help me forget my seasickness!'

I was most relieved to see that Mr Darwin had not gone mad, as my shipmates had reported. I was very glad to see him in such good spirits. However, his next comment made me think I was mistaken and, indeed, that he was out of his mind.

'Dust, George! Dust! Think of it!'

I couldn't understand what he was talking about. I was always most careful to dust. Keeping up with Mr Darwin and his untidy habits was no easy matter. Yet I feared the Captain with whom he shared the cabin. Captain FitzRoy was very particular about keeping things neat and shipshape, as he put it. I looked round for a duster but could not find one.

'Why, sir,' I cried, 'I dusted your cabin only last night.'

'Oh yes, I know that,' he replied, 'but the gunroom next door is full of dust. It came through the skylight.'

'But I dusted in there too. Captain FitzRoy ordered me to do so when I had finished in here.'

'You dusted the gunroom!' he cried in disbelief. 'Where did you put it?'

'Put it, sir? The dust, you mean?' I asked him.

'Of course, George, what else? Where did you put the dust?'

'Why sir, I put it where I always put it. I threw it overboard!'

Mr Darwin groaned. The look on his face was one of absolute dismay. 'You threw my dust overboard? I was going to collect samples this morning.'

He let out a sorrowful sigh. 'George, I know that you mean well. You are only a boy and I am forgetting the fact. Please accept my most sincere apology. I fear that I have not explained everything, properly, to you.'

Indeed, Mr Darwin had not explained things to me. Captain FitzRoy had given me the clearest orders. He did not want to see a speck of dust anywhere on board the ship. Mr Darwin, on the other hand, seemed to treasure the stuff.

'There will be other days, George, no doubt. Why, that last dust storm was something to behold. Did you see the poor sailors? It choked them and got into their eyes. Did you hear them sneeze?' he asked me.

'Yes, sir. I sneezed myself. With the greatest respect, Mr Darwin, why do you feel so fond of dust? After all, it is nothing very special surely?'

Mr Darwin fixed me with a steady stare. He sat me down and began to tell me of an idea that had recently been forming in his mind. We had been sailing through warm, tropical waters and, as I have already told you, we had approached the Equator. One day, the atmosphere clouded and the sun was nearly blotted out from view. However, the cloud that hid the sun was not one which brought rain. It was a dust cloud. Fine pieces, particles as they are called, had fallen from the sky to land on the deck of the Beagle. It was these particles that had caused the sailors so much distress.

Mr Darwin, unbeknown to me, had gone round the ship collecting dust and popping it into small paper envelopes which he had made. He called them his dust samples. Further, he explained to me that the dust cloud had travelled from land. I looked out through the porthole.

'You must be mistaken, sir. There's no land to be seen. The look-out on the crow's next would have shouted down to us.'

Mr Darwin smiled. He had forgiven me and I was glad of that.

'George, I tell you that this dust has travelled across the ocean from the nearest mainland. I had a word with Mr Wickham, the First Lieutenant. He told me that in this part of the ocean the winds blow from Africa, and that is a very long way from here. Africa is, in fact, more than three hundred miles away on our port bow. Don't you see, George? Don't you see what it means if dust can travel such distances?'

Frankly, I did not! I had no idea of what Mr Darwin was trying to tell me.

'Look at this, George! Under my microscope. Dust particles! I have mounted them on a small piece of glass.'

I went over to the brass microscope standing on the table. This was the first time I had been allowed to touch it. I screwed up one eye and with the other looked down the metal tube as best I could. Mr Darwin directed the light up the tube with a tiny, round mirror. I was told how to focus the picture and soon I realised that I was looking at small shapes of many colours. Some were grey, others were black and still others were tinged with green or brown.

'Look hard, now, George,' Mr Darwin told me. 'Examine! Use your eyes and discover what is to be seen. You are looking at dust, it is true, but there are other things to be seen. Tiny pieces of plants – spores we call them. Imagine! If they are borne on the wind all this way, from Africa, where will they end up?'

I looked up from the microscope. 'In the sea, Mr Darwin?' I asked.

'Eh! Oh yes that is true,' he replied. 'Indeed I suppose many of them will perish in the sea, but think of those that get blown onto islands. After all, there are islands out here, even in the middle of the Atlantic Ocean. Now, think! What would happen to one of these little African spores if it landed on the soil of a volcanic island?'

I had to think about the question. It seemed that these microscopic spores were a little like seeds.

'Would it grow, Mr Darwin? I mean would it develop into a plant?'

He clapped his hands with pleasure and beamed at me.

'We have the makings of a scientist in you, young George. A discoverer, and a thinker! Yes, indeed! Some of these tiny spores will grow into plants. Some will be fairly small in size, others will be large. Why, I expect there are pieces of giant fern tree here! This helps to explain how living things get from one place to another. Of course, it is easy for plants because the wind can carry their spores and seeds. But what about animals? Now there is a question for you.'

It was a very big question. I wonder, now, how I had not thought of it before. After all, we had already visited our first tropical island and had seen the wildlife for ourselves. This had happened a month before, on January 16th. Mr Darwin was very excited that day. It was to be his first chance to look at living tropical plants and animals.

We had dropped anchor off Porto Praya, a small town on St Jago, one of the Cape Verde Islands. Mr Darwin said that the island had been thrown up out of the sea by a volcano. Perhaps we expected to see great jungles growing up to the tops of the mountains. Whatever the case, it was not to be. There were enormous areas of black, volcanic lava which, many years ago, had erupted from the top of the mountain. Now, the island was cool and lifeless and scarcely anything grew on it. To be honest, I soon grew bored with it and returned to the ship. However, Mr Darwin and two of the officers hired ponies and rode some distance away from the coast. When he returned later in the day, he reported everything that had happened to him.

'Do you know, George, the native people have told us that it has not rained here for more than a year? Yet deep valleys have been carved out of the lava. This must happen after the occasional rainstorm when water rushes from the mountaintops down to the sea. At present, the dried up bushes in these valleys have no leaves. It is wonderful how nature manages to survive in these hot, dry conditions. I saw a kingfisher darting from a castor-oil plant to catch grasshoppers and lizards.

'On the other side of the island, at the village of

27

St Domingo, the scenery changes remarkably and it is truly beautiful. We arrived on a feastday and the black, native people sang and danced. A small, clear stream runs through the village and plants grow nearby. Everything is lush and green. I took the opportunity of examining the volcanic lava. How wonderful it is to see it here – where it belongs! I have made many notes for my book. Later, I shall write to my friends in England about it.

'Then, George, there is my greatest discovery of all, and I'm afraid Captain FitzRoy is not at all pleased with me!'

He pointed to the corner of the cabin where there was a barrel. I went over to it, lifted the lid and immediately sprang back in horror. The most revolting looking creature gazed up at me with a single eye. It was horribly slimy, and seemed to be all arms and legs. As I crashed the lid down in terror, the water swirled inside the barrel!

'Mr Darwin, what have you got in there? Is it a native god of some sort? It gives me the shivers and I shall not look at it again.'

Mr Darwin laughed out loud. 'I was becoming lonely, George. It is not much fun having only Captain FitzRoy for company so I decided to keep a pet. It's a delightful animal. It's called an octopus!'

An octopus? I had never heard of such a thing. 'Is it fish or fowl, Mr Darwin?' I asked him.

'Neither,' he replied. 'I suppose you could say that its nearest relatives on land are slugs and snails. That makes is a mollusc. Don't worry about such names, but let me tell you how I came to find it.'

Mr Darwin drew up a chair and began to tell me

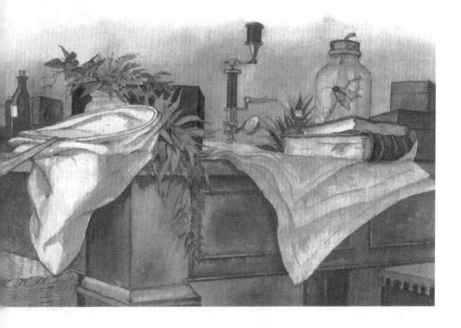

how he captured the octopus. He had gone down to the coast to examine rock pools. The octopus had got caught in one as the tide was going out. Evidently, it did not take to Mr Darwin. He told me how it backed away from him and dragged its body into a narrow crack in the rocks, using its long arms and suckers. These suckers helped it to fix fast and Mr Darwin explained how he had to pull and tug at the brute to shift it from its rocky lair.

'It seems to be a moody creature, George. Either it stays fast and will not come out, or it plays tricks on me. Why, it can even change colour! Before my very eyes I saw it change from a brownish purple to a yellowish green as it passed from deeper water to a shallow, sandy area. There it stayed for five minutes or so. Then I spied it venturing forward, inch by inch, changing colour as it crawled. Very slowly, I put a hand into the water and when I thought I could strike, I grabbed at the beast. Swoosh! At the speed of

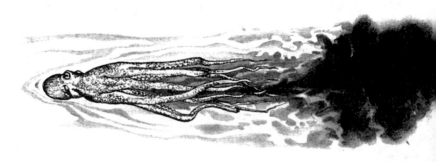

an arrow it flashed, head first, across the pool. I had no idea where it went, for in the pool there remained a cloud of deep brown ink, which spread through the water so thickly that I could see nothing else. What a remarkable escape act!'

'How did you finally capture the octopus, Mr Darwin?' I asked him.

'Skill, George!' he laughed. 'Sheer skill! After the creature had escaped I started crawling around the sides of the pool looking for it. It was then that I heard a sound. A small jet of water shot out making a grating noise as it did so. This was the octopus's giveaway sign. It is able to direct the jet of water which, I believe, may be something to do with the way in which it breathes. When it does this, you can see where it is hiding. With some effort, I grabbed him, popped him into a sack, and brought him back to the ship with me.'

Following the adventures on St Jago, Mr Darwin had been puzzled by a number of things. The recent dust storm and his exciting discoveries about what the dust contained made him think even more. It was all these thoughts which had made him so excited on this particular morning.

'You must excuse me now, George,' he said. 'I have much work to do.'

Boldly, I asked him what he intended to do, and if I could be of any help. His reply caused me to ponder a little.

'I wish to think, George. Just to think. I want to think about grasshoppers, lizards and kingfishers.'

That seemed little enough to think about! I asked him what he meant. He explained that he was somewhat puzzled. He told me to think back to the time the island was formed when the volcano erupted from the sea.

'Imagine it, George! What a sight it must have been. A raging furnace throwing dark clouds of ash high into the sky. Fiery sparks shooting up, then tumbling to the sea. Imagine the red hot lava pouring over the mouth of the volcano. Can you see a black mountain, on fire, rising out of the waves? Streams of molten rock gushing down its sides and sizzling at the sea's edge!'

It was a wonderful picture he painted.

'But Mr Darwin, what has that to do with lizards, grasshoppers and kingfishers. What are you suggesting? Do you believe that they, too, were born in the heart of the volcano?'

'A good question, George, and some people might believe that. I do not think so for one moment. That leaves me with a problem to solve. How is it that they got here on the island at all? We know that the seeds or spores of plants can be borne hundreds of miles on the wind. We think they come from Africa. So where did the lizards come from? For that matter, how did the grasshoppers get here? It's a very long jump from Africa. A few hundred miles or so! Answer me that one, George!'

Mr Darwin gets ants in his pants

On the last day of February 1832, our little warship reached the coast of South America and we put in at the port of Bahia, in Brazil. Mr Darwin was in a great hurry to be off and explore the delights that awaited him. It was my misfortune to stay on board the Beagle for most of this time and I was not often able to discover the excitements of the Brazilian forests for myself. All I could do, on this occasion, was to stand on deck and wave goodbye to the ship's boats as they pulled to the shore. Mr Darwin set out accompanied by members of the crew. Lieutenant Wickham was his closest companion on this trip. However, he preferred to spend only a short time on land and could not wait to return to the Beagle. How gladly I would have swopped places with him!

Mr Darwin came back laden with all kinds of exotic fruit. It was the first time I had seen a banana! The

sailors explained to me that it had to be peeled. They also told me about coconuts and how a hole had to be made in the hard shell in order to drink the milk. At first, I thought they were teasing me.

One day Lieutenant Wickham and Mr Darwin returned soaked to the skin. Mr Darwin explained.

'We were attacked, George! Attacked by natives. It's a mercy we escaped.'

I was very concerned about his adventure and asked him what had happened.

'It was the first day of the Carnival and Lieutenant Wickham, Mr Sullivan and I were determined to face its excitement. The village people have a wonderful time. They throw wax balls filled with water at each other. It is all very friendly and we could not help but

get mixed up with it. Poor old Wickham's naval uniform is in a dreadful state! To cap it all, the sky clouded over and we were soaked through by a heavy shower!'

Mr Darwin had great respect for the negro people. He found them graceful and courteous. They worked as slaves for their Portuguese owners, who, long ago, had conquered and settled in Brazil. Captain FitzRoy and Mr Darwin got into a fierce argument about slavery. It all started one morning when the Captain was in one of his black moods. I kept out of his way, as far as possible, and always knew when trouble was in store by the conversations of the sailors. They would ask each other how much 'hot coffee' had been served out that day. By that, they referred to the Captain's sharp and violent temper. This particular day was a hot coffee one! I was just about to enter the shared cabin when I heard the beginnings of a quarrel. Captain FitzRoy's voice was raised in anger.

'I will not have you disagree with me, Darwin,' he exploded. 'No officer or sailor dares to argue with me. Neither shall you!'

Mr Darwin was a brave soul and not easily frightened. 'FitzRoy,' he replied, 'I shall argue with you as I see fit! I have seen the black slave people and many of them are extremely badly treated. Slavery is a sin. Everything should be done to put a stop to it!'

Captain FitzRoy was nearly screaming with rage.

'I have just returned from the home of a Portuguese slave-owner and I was treated with great hospitality. My host brought his slaves to me and asked them if they were happy. They told him they were very happy to be with him. He asked them if they would wish to be free. "No," they replied. They did not wish for their freedom!'

Mr Darwin said that this was no way to get at the truth. Captain FitzRoy accused Mr Darwin of calling him a liar and said he no longer wished him to share his cabin. There was a cry of rage, and I fled from the door, just as it burst open and the Captain strode out. He was shaking with anger.

Later that day the officers offered Charles Darwin a place in their cabin. He was very grateful to them. Yet a curious thing happened. Captain FitzRoy calmed down, sent a massage of apology and invited Mr Darwin to return to the cabin. Peace was made, but that was only the first of many quarrels between the two men. I regretted this because I knew Mr Darwin to be a kindly and calm person and everyone got on well with him. As for the Captain, he was respected as a sailor and yet I believe that all those who sailed under him lived in fear of his dreadful moods and explosive temper. I do not believe that he could help these outbursts and perhaps was not even in control of them. However, it would also be unfair of me not to mention that at times he showed me, and others, great kindness and I will always remember him for this.

All I have just described happened in Bahia. During this time, Mr Darwin had much on his mind and he was very active. One day, he returned to the ship with ants in his pants. At least, that is what the sailors told me!

He had been travelling through the Brazilian jungle. 'George, we made our way into the forest. The trees grow nearly to blot out the sky from view and thick creepers hang from every branch. Beneath the trees I saw graceful ferns and many other bright green plants. Tiny humming birds darted round my head, pecking at brightly coloured flowers as they

sought their honeydew. Their wings beat so rapidly that it was nearly impossible to see them. Everywhere I went I found brilliant colours. Some were flowers and others were butterflies. There were such vivid blues and reds and oranges. In the shady parts, is a mixture of sound and silence. It is close to paradise, George!'

Mr Darwin was very impressed with the Brazilian rain forest. I listened in awe, then asked him about the ants.

'There is a small, dark-coloured ant, which can sometimes be seen travelling in great numbers. It was like watching an army on the march. They created panic in other creatures which got in their way and I spotted spiders, cockroaches, and lizards

that seemed to be in a terrible state of despair. They rushed across a bare piece of ground and not far behind them followed the ant army. Now the ants got ready for war and swarmed into battle lines. They completely surrounded the poor creatures. There was no escape! I experimented and placed a small stone in the way of one ant line. They closed in for the kill but soon retired. Another ant line came up and attacked my stone. As they could not destroy it, they gave up the battle and continued their march.'

Soon after this adventure, the Beagle sailed south and a few days later we arrived in Rio de Janeiro. The Beagle then continued its survey of the coast and I went with it, leaving Mr Darwin in a cottage at Rio. For the crew it was an unhappy voyage. Three of the sailors were stricken with fever and died. I missed Mr Darwin very much during the weeks we were away and I looked forward to our return to Rio. When we eventually got back, Mr Darwin was waiting for us and, as I expected, he had more tales to tell of his latest adventures.

'It is almost impossible to describe the beauty of the scenery, George. The forest is simply teeming with life. I found a little frog sitting on a blade of grass. When these frogs are close together they each make a different note so I could have formed a frog choir! They are very clever at climbing and I noticed that each tiny toe has a little sucker on it. This helps the frog to climb plants growing straight up from the ground. Why, I even had one climb a pane of glass for me!'

One thing I did not understand was why Mr Darwin was in the habit of giving animals fancy names. He wrote letters to his friends, but he never wrote about a 'blue butterfly' or a 'striped butterfly' he had found. He gave them names like *Rhetus periander* (that was a blue butterfly). He also talked about *Diaethria meridionalis*, which is a white butterfly with black circles and markings on its wings. I asked him why he always used long and complicated names.

'My friends need to know exactly which butterfly I am writing about, George. Why, there must be hundreds of different blue butterflies, here! Each kind has a special name in Latin, so everyone understands which butterfly I mean. As we give them Latin names, it means that scientists in different countries and speaking different languages also understand which butterfly I am writing about. They learn Latin just as we do. So it is a language that we share between us.'

He must have noticed the puzzled expression on my face. It did not seem to make much sense to me. I knew no Latin! He laughed sympathetically and patted me on the shoulder.

'Poor young George! There is so much to learn and we can never come to the end of it. It is just the same for me. That is what makes life so exciting!'

Perhaps life was exciting for Mr Darwin, but for me Latin was one more difficulty. I had started to learn to read and write English on the voyage. One of the officers helped me and also set exercises for me to do. You will remember that I had never been to school. By the end of our journey I could read perfectly.

I was beginning to become a bit of a scientist, too, and Mr Darwin was very pleased with me. My first attempt at being a scientist took place after the Beagle returned to Rio de Janeiro. Along with a small party of sailors, I visited an orange grove. Fluttering above my head was a small butterfly and, as I began to watch it, it landed on a tree trunk near to my head. Then I noticed another one. This, too, landed upon the same trunk. Like the other one, it landed and remained upside-down with its beautiful wings spread out. I thought I would catch one for Mr Darwin and so, very slowly, I approached the trunk. I was just about to place my hand over the butterfly when it shuffled to one side. I tried again but once more, it dodged my hand and moved out of the way!

Mr Darwin was most interested when I told him about it on my return to the ship. Next day, we returned together to the orange grove, where even he had the greatest difficulty in collecting a specimen.

When we were leaving the orange grove a curious thing happened. I realised, more than ever, just how interested Mr Darwin was in the plants and animals he studied. The orange grove was on the edge of the forest and just after we started our journey back to the Beagle, a huge brown and black butterfly flapped lazily away into the forest trees. Mr Darwin grabbed a net from my hand and leapt after the monstrous insect in great excitement, leaving me to follow as best I could. It was several minutes before I caught up with him. When I finally did, it was to see the big brown and black creature winging its way up into the tree tops, leaving Mr Darwin mopping his brow with a large red and white spotted handkerchief. As I approached him, he flopped down on a fallen tree trunk and beckoned me to join him.

As we were about to get up after a short rest, I noticed a large black beetle crawl out from underneath a piece of rotten bark on the trunk. I drew Mr Darwin's attention to it and he immediately caught the beetle in his right hand. However, no sooner was the creature caught in his grasp than a second much more brightly coloured beetle appeared from the same spot. Quick as a flash, Mr Darwin grasped this second insect in his other hand. It was while he was examining both specimens very intently that a third and even bigger and more brightly coloured beetle appeared. Mr Darwin was determined not to let this third insect escape, so he popped the beetle in his right hand into his mouth, thus releasing his hand to capture the third one. After I had helped him to put the first two beetles into collecting boxes, he removed the third beetle from his mouth. I was frightened it might have poisoned Mr Darwin but it did him no harm. However, it did produce a nasty tasting fluid which Mr Darwin suggested might be used to stop other animals eating the beetle if it was caught. He said he might have to try tasting more beetles to find out if they also produced the same type of fluid!

Gunfire, revolution and men overboard

It was now time to leave Rio de Janeiro with its fine harbour and sugarloaf mountain. As we continued south, I was excited to see porpoises leaping over the waves. There were hundreds of them and they cut across our bows as bold as could be. Mr Darwin was very interested in their movements which he studied with great curiosity. Finally we reached a great river mouth. You could see mud in the water carried down from the river.

'The River Plate, George!'

'River Plate, sir?' I asked him. 'That is a peculiar name for a river.'

Mr Darwin grinned. 'All right, George. You have asked for it. First, you grumble when I speak to you in Latin. Now, I must speak to you in Spanish. We shall call it Rio de la Plata. It is an enormous river mouth. Look, here it is on the map.' We stood at the ship's rail and examined the map.

'There are two great rivers which run into the Rio de la Plata. One is the River Paraná and the other the River Uruguay. On the south side of the Rio de la Plata is Buenos Aires which is the great city of Argentina. On the north side is Montevideo and that is where we are bound for next. Between the two cities lies this enormous river mouth. It is miles wide!'

At about three o'clock that afternoon, I noticed a heavy gathering of black clouds to the south-west. The breeze grew stronger and gathered force and we were obliged to take in our light sails. Shafts of lightning flashed across the sky and Captain FitzRoy looked very grim.

'It is the pampero,' he explained, 'the local storm. I have been here before and I know what it can do!' As he spoke, the clouds darkened further and another bolt of lightning arched ahead of us.

'Shorten sail!' commanded the Captain. He ordered the topsail and foresail to be taken in.

At this moment the ship was struck by a tremendous wind. She keeled over and only just righted herself. But suddenly the Beagle was out of control! She was not answering her helm.

Mr Darwin joined me on the deck. Outwardly, he looked calm, but underneath I think he was as frightened as me. As we grasped the rail, we looked aloft to see the sailors on the yardarms. They were hanging on for dear life. The sea blew up and the ship pitched and rolled.

'We are lost, Mr Darwin,' I cried. 'Dear God, save us!'

He shouted back to me but in the screaming of the wind I could not hear him. At this moment, we heard a sickening crack and our mainmast snapped like a piece of tinder wood. The sails were now in tatters yet, curiously, the brave little boat responded and the helmsman regained control. Now, we were all clinging on desperately. Huge spars, splintered and ruined, fell crashing down on the deck which was covered with the remains of the sails. The scene was chaotic. Above the howling wind we heard a piercing scream and ducking to avoid a falling spar, I watched, helplessly, as a young sailor fell from the maintopsail. His body was hurled out to the raging sea. We felt so useless and could offer him little help. However, he was a strong swimmer and the poor fellow bobbed up and down on the seething waves. Some of the other sailors threw him a life-buoy and pieces of broken timber. Yet, it was to no avail. Eventually, he gave up his struggle and sank out of sight. We learned, later, that a second sailor had also fallen from the yardarm and lost his life. Captain FitzRoy was dreadfully upset and took the blame himself.

'I should have anchored and ridden out the storm,' he told Mr Darwin later as they drank coffee together in the cabin. 'I was a fool to try to make for port.'

Mr Darwin attempted to comfort him. In truth, Captain FitzRoy had saved our lives and there was not a sailor aboard who did not admire him for his knowledge of the sea. That night and all through the next day, the crew worked to repair the damage.

It was 26th July. We had just come into the bay at Montevideo and were about to anchor when we received signals from another British warship, the frigate Druid.

The first signal read: 'Clear for action.' The second one read: 'Prepare to cover our boats.'

The British warship was asking for our help and the Beagle's sailors got ready and mounted their guns. Shortly, six small boats from Druid crammed with sailors in blue jackets, passed us. Their small boat guns were mounted. We gave them cover as they headed towards the port of Montevideo. One of the officers told me that some of these South American countries were always getting themselves into trouble. It seemed that the new governor of the country had stolen four hundred horses belonging to a British resident. Naturally he was very angry about this and had asked for help from the British Navy. Just to make matters more confused, it appeared that the governor of the city who had seized the horses

was also under attack from another army. He faced the British Navy coming in from the sea and a small enemy force on the other side of the city!

We left them to it and sailed farther up the River Plate towards the great city of Buenos Aires on the southern bank. This would be our first sight of the country of Argentina. We sailed close to the city and, in order to obtain a better view, I climbed to the top of the mainmast. A little way off, I saw an old gunship and I could not believe my eyes when I spotted a puff of smoke billow out from her side. It was followed by a muffled bang. Nothing else happened and we sailed on. Then there was a second puff of smoke and a louder bang. A cannonball flew straight for my head! Desperately clinging to the yardarm, I ducked just as the missile passed over. It fell into the sea beyond the ship. Captain FitzRoy took no action, but continued sailing and soon we had passed out of range. Some miles farther on we put down our

anchor, and it was not long before two of our ship's boats put out to sail to the landing place. In one of them I spied Mr Darwin.

After a while the boats returned to the ship as they had not been allowed to land at Buenos Aires. Captain FitzRoy was in a fury. It turned out that the Spanish-speaking Argentinians feared that we might bring with us the dreaded disease, cholera, and this was why they had fired upon us! It had been a warning shot. Captain FitzRoy sent the governor of Buenos Aires a strong message, protesting at their rude behaviour. He also sent a message to the Captain of the gunship that had fired at us.

We loaded our guns and this time sailed close to the Argentinian gunship. Captain FitzRoy hailed the Argentinian ship and warned that he would blast her out of the water should she fire so much as a single shot at us. Needless to say, she did not dare!

Now, all that seemed excitement enough for one voyage, but it was not quite over yet! We returned to Montevideo to find the city in a turmoil. A party of soldiers had rebelled against the governor. He sent a message to the Beagle asking for help. Captain FitzRoy went ashore and an hour or so later signalled to us to follow him in the boats. Immediately, the sailors sprang into action. Our ship's boats, the yawl, cutter, whaleboat and gig were put to sea. More than fifty of us climbed into them although I was not supposed to have been there! We were armed with pistols, muskets and cutlasses and, on our arrival on shore, we marched bravely to the fort. There we camped and, as the sun set for the night, we cooked enormous beefsteaks. All was quiet in the town but we knew that the rebel soldiers had mounted artillery guns in the streets.

We had to take special care because only a few sailors had been left aboard the Beagle. They kept watch through the night for fear of being boarded. Next day, we learned that the rebel soldiers had gathered in another fortress in the city. To their dismay, they were surrounded by a great crowd of townspeople and they could not escape! The revolution fizzled out and became more of a carnival for everyone to enjoy. We had had enough of those silly goings-on and so returned to our ship. Soon, as Captain FitzRoy explained, our real work was to begin. The British Admiralty had commanded him to survey the South American coast south of the River Plate.

Jemmy Button returns to the Land of Fire

Aboard our ship were three people very different from the rest of the crew. They came from a country called Tierra del Fuego, which means Land of Fire. Their dark skins and narrow eyes were unlike those of the English sailors and they looked very strange in the clothes that they were forced to wear. Even their names were peculiar. One was called Jemmy Button, another was York Minster and the third was a young woman called Fuegia Basket. During the voyage, they became my friends. Jemmy called me 'Poor, poor fellow' when I became seasick and during these occasional periods of illness he comforted me as best he could. It was not always easy to understand him but he told me some astonishing tales about Captain FitzRoy.

The first thing I learned was that Captain FitzRoy had sailed in South American waters before. About four years previously, he had taken the Beagle down to the very southernmost tip of the continent. There he had a lot of trouble from the people who lived on the island of Tierra del Fuego. The Fuegians, as they were called, were hardy and very fierce. They stole from the ship's boats which landed on their shores. Jemmy told me that the Captain had become very angry with them and had taken some hostages. Captain FitzRoy told the leaders of the Fuegians that he would sail away with his hostages and return them only if the thieving stopped. The leaders did not seem to care. The Fuegians continued their stealing and Captain FitzRoy, true to his promise, sailed back to England with his four hostages.

The Captain had great plans for his captives. He had decided that they should receive a proper education and that their souls should be saved by converting them to Christianity. Very soon, however, the plan began to go wrong. One of them, Boat Memory, caught smallpox and quickly died. The other, three were sent to a vicar in London to begin their education. Captain FitzRoy then had another idea for his great plan. When their education was complete he would sail back to the Land of Fire with his three captured Fuegians and return them to their homeland. The three new Christians could then live among their own people and tell them about God and Jesus. The King and Queen heard about this idea and commanded Captain FitzRoy to show them his Fuegian friends. Their majesties were very gracious and pleased when the Captain told them that he would ask an English missionary to return with Jemmy, York and Fuegia and that this missionary would work alongside them in spreading the Christian message. That is how Mr Matthews, the missionary, and the three Fuegians came to be on board H.M.S. Beagle when I joined the ship at the start of the voyage.

'Master George,' spoke Jemmy. 'You not like our Land of Fire. It is full of fierce storms and we have much thunder. Truly, you will be afraid.'

For some months we explored the coastline of South America. We saw Patagonia but finally headed for the far south. Jemmy Button, York Minster and Fuegia Basket were going home! One week before Christmas we entered Good Success Bay and Jemmy gazed upon his homeland. Although we were still

51

some days' travel from his own people, there were tears in his eyes. For my part, I did not like the look of it at all. We had sailed along a rugged, rocky coastline. A dark forest grew down from the mountains behind the shore and we could not see the mountaintops which were swathed in thick, grey cloud. Rain swept off the mountains and the wind blew hard. We were glad to have reached the sheltered harbour of Good Success Bay.

All the same I was afraid. A small party of Fuegians had been following the progress of our ship and, occasionally, they let out wild cries which echoed off the hilltops. Now and again, we spied them scampering through the forest at the sea's edge. I felt that our missionary would have a difficult task ahead of him.

Next morning, we put out a boat and went ashore. I sat next to Mr Darwin. He looked nervous, as did some of the sailors and Mr Matthews. Jemmy, a great friend of Mr Darwin, was with us, too. Even he did not look as happy as I had expected. Captain FitzRoy bit his lip and tapped his fingers nervously on the side of the boat. Four Fuegians awaited us on the shore and as we pulled close to them, one began to shout and waved his arms.

'He say where to land,' explained Jemmy. 'This man is their chief.'

We jumped out of the boat and heaved it up on the beach. The four Fuegians were startling in appearance. They were very tall and their skins were the colour of dull red copper. Their hair was long and black and very entangled. The chief was an old man with two bands of colour painted on his face. A bright red band stretched from one ear to the other and above that he had painted a white band. Even his eyelids were white.

'Good gracious, George!' exclaimed Mr Darwin.
'They're devils! Look at the others.

How they glared at us! Their faces were streaked with black charcoal and one of them had a white band across his eyes, like the chief. Captain FitzRoy was very bold. He had brought a present for them. It was a gift of pieces of scarlet cloth and was much to their liking. At once, we were friends and they tied the cloth around their necks. One of the Fuegians approached me making a clucking noise with his tongue, and grinned hideously. The next thing I knew was that I was bowled over on my back and I lay winded from the fall. The Fuegian had struck me a blow in the chest. A sailor raised his fist and ran to protect me.

'No! No!' shouted Jemmy in alarm. 'He is a friend. He is a good man!'

The Fuegian picked me up and patted me on the chest, only this time he was a little more gentle.

'This is his way of saying hello,' explained Jemmy. 'It is like a handshake.'

While this was taking place, Mr Darwin was having his chest patted by the chief! Then the old man pulled his skin cloak to one side and invited Mr Darwin to slap him back. They understood one another perfectly and soon they were laughing together.

'Let's give them a song!' cried Robert Hammond, our ship's mate.

Very soon, we were all dancing and singing at the tops of our voices. What a strange sight it must have been, Mr Darwin, Captain FitzRoy and the rest of the crew dancing with the Fuegians on a lonely beach, many thousands of miles from our homeland.

Poor Jemmy Button did not have things so easy. The Fuegians were greatly puzzled by him. In his way, he was as different from them as he was from us. The chief spoke for a long time with him but Jemmy told me later that he had difficulty understanding what was said. They were from different parts of Tierra del Fuego and from different tribes. Jemmy also felt ashamed of his countrymen as he found them so savage. Poor Jemmy had very mixed feelings. He realised that he was not really one of us, yet was no longer one of them and this saddened him greatly.

Next day, Mr Darwin, Jemmy and I set off to explore the surrounding country. We took food and drink with us and I carried Mr Darwin's collecting boxes. By midday we were tired and depressed. We had pushed our way into the thick overgrown forest

of beech trees but it was not like the tropical jungles of Brazil. Here all was gloom and dullness, and dying trees rotted away on the forest floor which was soaking with dampness. We discovered a mountain stream and, with the greatest difficulty, made our way up the mountain to the edge of the forest. Here we gazed on a wet, barren area of swamp beyond which we could see the tops of snow-covered mountains.

Our spirits were very low as we imagined trying to live here. It was a land of gales, driving rain, sleet and thick gloomy cloud. We returned to the ship later in the day and were glad to be among our friends once again. I felt better in the warmth and safety of Mr Darwin's cabin whose familiar contents gave me a feeling of security.

Christmas Day, 1832, found us anchored not far from Cape Horn at the very southernmost tip of South America. There were many small islands around Cape Horn and we were fortunate not to be blown upon their rocky shores. Lieutenant Sullivan had warned me of Cape Horn and told me stories of shipwrecked mariners. We had sailed into the 'teeth' of the wind through mountainous waves while heavy squalls of rain swept across the ship from the low black clouds. Lieutenant Sullivan described the weather conditions as the worst in the world. It was there we spent our Christmas at Wigwam Cove, a

little bay sheltered from the weather. The native Fuegians visited the bay to hunt for shellfish on the rocks by the sea and it was there that we discovered the remains of one of their wigwams.

Some days later, we sailed to Wollaston Island. There we spotted a canoe with six naked Fuegians in it. It was cold and rainy and I have never in my life seen more miserable-looking people. They had not bothered to make a wigwam and slept out at night in the rain with no protection. I never fancied their food which was mostly shellfish from the rocks or horrid berries from bushes. However, occasionally they managed to kill a seal or even found the rotting body of a whale washed up on the beach and this provided them with plenty of food for many days.

'These people fierce, Master George,' Jemmy told me. 'You be careful. They eat you!'

I did not believe him.

'It true, Master George. Sometimes they have no food. They eat their dogs. But first they eat old ladies!'

'Do you mean that they are cannibals, Jemmy?' I asked in horror.

'Yes, Master George. Old women run away to forest when there is no food. Men chase them and kill them. They eat. When no more old women, they eat dogs.'

I could not understand why anyone ate old women before their dogs.

'Dogs good. They hunt animals. They kill otter. Make good fur for clothing,' Jemmy explained. 'Sometimes, tribes make war. They eat each other. It is true!'

Mr Darwin had been listening very attentively to this conversation.

'I fear for our missionary, George. Poor Mr Matthews, I hope he will survive. He may end up as someone's dinner!'

Jemmy Button had few doubts.

'Mr Matthews, he be eaten. He not understand. He think God save him. These people not know God. They like eat him!'

Mr Darwin and I looked at each other and feared the worst. On December 30th we set sail once more. Now we would round Cape Horn and explore the west coast of Tierra del Fuego.

In mid-January, we sighted an enormous mountain. The famous explorer Captain Cook had named this York Minster, after the great cathedral in England. Now I knew how our Fuegian friend had been given this peculiar name. York was going home with the gentle and kind Fuegia and soon they would become man and wife. After a violent storm, we dropped anchor at Ponsonby Sound. Four boats were equipped to sail up a channel which had been discovered by Captain FitzRoy on his last voyage. The channel lay between high chains of mountains and Captain FitzRoy had named it the Beagle Channel.

Jemmy Button became excited because this was his true homeland. Fires on shore were lit by Fuegians spreading the news of our arrival and one party waved sticks and shouted and screamed at us ferociously. Nevertheless, a little way up the channel, we landed and a hostile group came down to the shore. We gave them small presents of red cloth and biscuits. They tied the bright red material around their heads and then demanded the silver buttons on our coats. In fact, they wanted everything! Jemmy grew more and more ashamed of his own people.

We camped for the night but soon realised that the Fuegians were beginning to grow bolder. When Captain FitzRoy flashed his sword at them, they only laughed. Some held stones in their hands, ready to attack us and smash our skulls. Captain FitzRoy even fired his musket, but this caused them no fear because they did not understand that it could kill them. However, we survived the night and, next day, continued our journey along the Beagle Channel where forests grew down to the water's edge and high, jagged mountains broke the skyline.

The next night, a small group of Tekenika people arrived. Their bodies were naked, save for the colours of painted decorations, and they looked like multi-coloured demons! These were Jemmy Button's own people and they accompanied us down the Beagle Channel to Woollya's Cove, where Jemmy's mother and family lived.

The land was better at this spot. We built three large wigwams and it was decided that missionary Matthews and Jemmy would stay there. After some discussion York and Fuegia also decided to join them and not return to their own people further to the west. For five days we worked hard, making gardens for them and sowing seeds. Also, Captain FitzRoy gave them boxes of equipment and plenty of provisions.

On the morning of January 24th, it appeared that the whole of Jemmy's tribe had arrived. His mother and brothers came, too. I looked forward to the reunion between the members of the family but poor Jemmy was to be disappointed. His mother simply stared at him and after a while walked away. Jemmy tried to talk to his brothers but found that he had all but forgotten their language. Nevertheless, apart from this sad blow, all else seemed to be well. Over a hundred Fuegians helped us to build Mr Matthews' encampment or, rather, the women did the hard work whilst the menfolk sat and watched!

Three days after our arrival at Woolya's Cove a strange thing happened. The women and children disappeared and hid in the surrounding forest. Fearing a surprise attack Captain FitzRoy decided to leave and make camp a few miles away. Mr Matthews, however, was exceedingly brave. He trusted in God and decided to stay along with Jemmy, York and Fuegia. Bidding farewell for the night, we left them and returned next morning. All was peaceful and well, so Captain FitzRoy decided to carry out further explorations but promised to return to Woolya's Cove, in due course. We took to our boats, waving to Mr Matthews and our Fuegian friends, and did not return for nearly a week.

When we got back, Mr Matthews was a shaken and saddened man for he had been given a very bad time by Jemmy's people. They had surrounded him night and day and he had to keep constant watch because of their thieving. They had threatened him with sticks and stones and he had given them everything he had. Captain FitzRoy ordered Mr Matthews to accompany him back to the Beagle but Jemmy, York and the gentle Fuegia were left to fend for themselves.

One year later, in March 1834, we returned to Woollya's Cove but found it deserted. As we were about to depart, we spotted a canoe paddling towards us. In it was a thin, untidy Fuegian, his hair filthy and entangled. He was desperately trying to wash paint from his face. When the canoe came nearer, we realised that we were looking at our old friend Jemmy Button. It was a great shock. However, he tidied himself up and later that night brought his new, young wife to meet us. Mr Darwin asked Jemmy about York Minster and Fuegia but Jemmy spat on the ground. Jemmy told us that York had stolen all his belongings and, taking Fuegia with him, had set off by canoe to join his own tribe.

Our ship set sail up the Beagle Channel to return to the sea and continue our voyage. As we departed, Jemmy watched us from the shore and lit a fire. It was his way of saying farewell and, as we rounded the headland, a plume of white smoke rose above the trees. We were never to see Jemmy again.

Cowboys and Indians

South America is such an enormous land! It is made of a number of countries, many of which we were able to visit on our long voyage. One of our explorations took place soon after we had returned Jemmy, Fuegia and York to their native land. Instead of carrying on up the west coast, Captain FitzRoy decided to round the Cape once more and return to Buenos Aires. We passed the forbidding coastline of Patagonia and, in August 1833, we anchored in the Rio Negro. This is a large river flowing down to the sea from a broad valley. Mr Darwin sought permission from Captain FitzRoy to disembark and travel the five hundred miles overland to Buenos Aires. There he would meet up with the Beagle and rejoin the ship's company.

I longed to go with my friend and as soon as I heard of his plan, I decided to leave the Beagle myself and join him on his overland journey. I helped Mr Darwin to pack his luggage and his collecting equipment but before he took leave of the Captain I secretly slipped away from the ship. Mr Darwin had arranged to meet an Englishman called Mr Harris at the nearby town of Patagones. They planned to travel together with a guide and five rough-looking cowboys who were known as gauchos. I followed Mr Darwin to Patagones and, as the party saddled their horses in preparation for their journey, I dared to make my appearance. Mr Darwin was shocked!

'George! Good gracious, boy, what on earth are you doing here?' he cried, eyeing me with astonishment. 'You should be with the Beagle, young man. Be of with you. Run or you'll miss the ship!'

I felt very embarrassed. Eight grown men stared down at me from their horses.

'I cannot go back to the ship, sir. It has already sailed,' I told him.

Mr Darwin groaned.

'Harris, I apologise to you, sir. This young rascal has a mind of his own. What Captain FitzRoy will have to say when he sees him again I cannot imagine. He'll skin him alive I shouldn't wonder!'

Mr Harris looked hard at me with steely eyes. 'The boy's a deserter, Darwin. He has left a ship of the Royal Navy. He will be severely punished – flogged at the very least!'

I stood there, looking up at them, feeling small and very afraid.

'The boy will have to come with us for now, continued the Englishman. He shouted in Spanish to one of the gauchos, who gave me a fiercesome look with his dark eyes. The gaucho jumped off his horse and went to saddle one of the spare horses in the party.

'Can you ride, boy?' enquired Mr Harris.

'No, sir,' I replied. 'I've never been on a horse.'

Mr Harris chuckled and spoke in Spanish once more to the gauchos. They roared with laughter and Mr Darwin seemed amused, too.

'Now is the time to learn, young man,' Mr Harris told me. 'By the end of the day you're going to be saddle-sore. And you'll thoroughly deserve it!'

A gaucho pulled on the reins of his horse, which I thought was about to trample me. He then bent over and pulled me up with one strong arm and, spurring his horse, rode over to the newly saddled one and dropped me heavily across its back. A roar of laughter went up from the travellers as I worked my seat into the saddle and struggled to stay on.

In a series of fits and starts I managed to tag along behind the experienced horsemen and by nightfall I felt so bruised and stiff that I longed for the comfort of the Beagle. Even Captain FitzRoy's temper would have been less punishment than this!

Next day, stiff with pain, I struggled once more into the saddle and rode all day gazing at the surrounding countryside. It was a dry, dusty and boring land which rose a little in places and dipped in others. Withered brown grass attempted to grow in wiry patches amongst low bushes bearing thorns. The horses were watered at a well of unpleasant-smelling water which we were warned not to drink. Our water was carried in leather bottles and was strictly rationed. Never in my life have I been so thirsty.

Ahead of us we saw a tree on a patch of high ground. Our gaucho companions drew out their guns as we approached it and all the while they searched the immediate countryside for signs of Indians. Mr Harris told Mr Darwin that we were about to pass the alter of the Indian God Waleechu. When we got to the tree, we found that its leafless, thorny branches were much decorated with little offerings. Tied on by threads were small pieces of bread and meat, pieces of cloth and the occasional cigar! It was then that we noticed, around the base of the tree, the bones of horses bleached by exposure to the sun. Mr Darwin got down to inspect them.

'We cannot wait too long, Darwin,' called Mr Harris. 'We risk attack at this spot.'

Mr Darwin reluctantly remounted his horse. He spoke to a gaucho who understood English.

'He tells me that Indians slaughter their horses here as sacrifices,' he explained.

'Ride on, sir,' commanded Mr Harris anxiously, who knew that the gauchos were becoming restless as they nervously fingered their guns.

'I wish to camp as far away as possible from here,' he went on. 'It will grow dark soon and we are most likely being watched by Indians, even now.

We continued on our way. The horses were tired after their exhausting day and seemed relieved, as we were, when Mr Harris gave orders to stop and make camp. At that moment, a shout went up from two of the gauchos who kicked their horses into a gallop. They fairly flew over the ground and I saw them twirling their lassos in pursuit of something which I could not see beyond the cover of the thorn bushes.

They soon returned in triumph, pulling along a poor cow which must have strayed from the herd of the nearest ranch. The cow's eyes rolled in misery and the gauchos quickly slaughtered the wretched creature in front of us. Branches of thorns were gathered to make a fire and before long I had forgotten my concern for the cow and was tucking into a juicy steak! We ate like kings but I noticed that Mr Harris had organised the gauchos to take turns in standing guard. Any wild Indians in the area would have had to be deaf and blind not to be aware of our presence.

Next morning, we broke camp and set off once more. My stiffness had eased considerably and I was getting into the way of this outdoor gaucho life. We had been travelling for about an hour, when suddenly, Mr Darwin raised a cry.

'George! George! To your right – look!'

I stood up in my stirrups and craned my neck to see over the tops of the nearby bushes.

'Whoa!' shouted Mr Harris and we all pulled up our horses.

'Guanacos, George,' said Mr Darwin in excitement. 'They are wild llamas.'

I had never seen such creatures. There were about a dozen of them staring at us and I was struck by their elegance and, in particular, by their long, thin necks. One of them raised its head a little and neighed a high note of alarm. The others replied to what was perhaps the leader of the herd. Quite slowly, they moved off, keeping a wary eye on us. Our gauchos were keen to hunt one for sport, but Mr Harris forbade them to do so. Then the guanacos began to canter and moved away in line, along a dusty path through the bushes. I was feeling glad that we were not to pursue them when, all of a sudden, panic broke out among the herd. They neighed shrilly and seemed to race about in all directions although it was

difficult to see what had happened because of the dust they kicked up. Suddenly, one gaucho grabbed his gun and raised it to his shoulder. I squinted through the dust at the scattered herd and, to my horror, saw a lion clawing at the shoulder of one of the llamas.

'Don't shoot!' cried Mr Darwin. 'Don't shoot, man!'

'But . . . is lion, Meester Darwin. I shoot . . . yes? asked the gaucho.

'No!' cried Mr Darwin. 'Let nature take its own course!' The gaucho lowered his gun very reluctantly and moodily rode slowly forward.

As we proceeded on our way, Mr Darwin explained that the animal we had seen attacking the herd was a puma – a South American lion. To this day, I believe that it had not spotted us, so keen was it on hunting its prey. Pumas, I was told, are very cunning, intelligent animals. Later on the journey, we were to discover more signs of them when we came across llama skeletons littered over the ground. Their necks had been broken in the fight with their greatest enemy. Mr Darwin was able to find foot-prints of pumas, some of them very fresh, but the llama attack was the only time I actually saw one for myself. The gaucho who had been ordered not to fire

grew extraordinarily sulky. His pride had been insulted as he would not now be able to boast about a brave kill to his comrades. For my part, I was happy to let the puma live.

Towards dusk that day, we made our camp and a fire of brushwood was lit. Soon after our evening meal, the gaucho who had been upset came quietly up to me and smiled.

'Master George, I teach you hunting? We go find good sport? We find plenty game . . . yes?'

I was not anxious to accompany him but, as I looked at the long deadly knife stuck inside his belt, I decided that I had better not refuse. The other gauchos had struck up a song and no-one had spotted his movements in the dim light.

'We go,' he said. 'Make secret. Not tell others. Come!'

So saying, Eduardo, for that was his name, and I slid silently away from our camp in the gathering dusk. We bent low to keep our heads below the line of the thorns and made our way to where the horses were grazing. Silently he lifted me up onto his horse then jumped up himself, and we rode together, bareback, away from the camp. Our departure was not noticed and when we were some distance away, Eduardo laughed.

'We find big birds. We find puma. Eduardo, he good hunter!'

We had been riding for only a few minutes, when suddenly, there was a whirring sound coming at us through the air. Our horse reared and plunged, whinnying with fear, as something struck the lower part of its hind leg.

Eduardo clutched onto its mane and I clung onto him as the frightened beast plunged through the

68

bushes. Thorns tore into my flesh and into the sides of the horse, but our mad dash continued, out of control. A spear sailed between my head and that of Eduardo, quickly followed by another. Our horse stumbled and fell and we crashed to the ground, badly winded and very frightened. Eduardo screamed as a third spear pierced his chest killing him instantly. I scrambled quickly for cover as a small party of Indians dashed upon him from the near darkness. Perhaps they had not seen me in the gloom and thought that only one rider was upon the horse. Whatever the case, I shall never know. The Indians raced after the horse, which was now lame, and quickly captured it. In no time, they disappeared into the shrubland leaving me lying on the ground, shaking and terrified, my heart pounding with fear.

About one hour later, I stumbled back to the glow of our camp fire, and the wrath of Mr Harris and Mr Darwin. They had heard the commotion somewhere out in the thorns, and truly, they were furious with me. The other gauchos crowded round asking about their comrade and I did my best to explain what had happened. Mr Darwin saw that I was terrified and had come close to losing my life.

'George, you're a young scoundrel. Whenever will you learn? You already have the grave anger of Captain FitzRoy to face and here, with us, you have acted most foolishly. Yet you're a brave boy, for all that, and I suppose Eduardo was really to blame, poor fellow.'

Mr Harris nodded sadly. 'He had a wife and family at my ranch,' he said. 'This is sad news, indeed.'

I was asked to give a full account of everything that had happened but the part that I could not explain was the whirring noise I had heard. Also, I was at a loss to explain why our horse had so suddenly gone lame. It was a mystery to me.

'There is a simple explanation, George,' Mr Harris said to me. 'Those Indians have been tracking us ever since we started out. They hate the white man and everything he stands for because they have been driven off their lands. There is a soldier whose name is General Rosas and it is his aim to kill every Indian –

man, woman and child. Even now, his army is out hunting not many miles from here. Some of the Indians surrender and live miserable lives in the service of the white man but most choose to fight. Soon enough, they will be cleared from this land which we are now passing through. The Indians who attacked you and Eduardo were patiently waiting for an opportunity to have a go at us. They are skilled hunters and have invented a weapon called a bolas. See here!' He opened a leather bag and showed the strange but very deadly instrument.

'The indians use three stones, two of them about the size of an apple. The other is a little smaller. Do you see how they are joined together by these tough, leather thongs?'

In the light of the camp fire, I looked to see how the three stones were attached to each other.

'One of the stones is held in the hand as the others are whirled about the head. Suddenly, the bolas is let go. It speeds towards its target which may be the neck of a llama or indeed the leg of an enemy's horse. When the bolas strikes, the stones and thongs wrap themselves around the part of the animal they have hit and may break its neck or leg.'

I realised how fortunate I had been to escape capture and perhaps death. Poor Eduardo's family would no longer have a father to fend for them and I felt that in some way I was to blame. I slept little that night under the stars and when I did sleep, my dreams were or whirring bolases and flying spears.

Giant birds and wild cats

Some days after our adventures in wild Indian country, we reached the village of Bahia Blanca. I was much relieved to see its fortified walls which, for increased protection, had been surrounded by a deep water-ditch. Soldiers mounted guard on the walls and eyed us with some suspicion as we rode through the main gate. This was immediately closed behind us and, as we looked around, the dirty little houses seemed to our party like havens of peace. However, the village lay under constant threat from Indian tribes in the neighbourhood because the government had taken their land. Nevertheless, during our short stay there, we made one or two excursions into the countryside.

I was very nervous during my stay in the village because I knew that the Beagle was expected to arrive there at the end of August. As you may imagine, I was filled with foreboding at the thought of meeting up with Captain FitzRoy. In my mind I had formed a plan but it was something I kept entirely to myself and I did not tell anyone, not even Mr Darwin. If Captain FitzRoy was determined to punish me in the way Mr Harris described, I would run away and become a gaucho!

On August 24th we spied the white sails of the Beagle as she lay at anchor in the harbour. I accompanied the welcoming party to greet Captain FitzRoy as he came ashore. After shaking hands with Mr Darwin and Mr Harris, Captain FitzRoy turned to face me with a grim expression.

'I'm surprised to see you here boy! It was my understanding that you deserted our ship!'

Without giving me time to answer he ordered my arrest, and I was quickly dragged away by one of the sailors of the landing party. As I was forced into the small boat to return to the Beagle, I turned to see Captain FitzRoy and Mr Darwin arguing furiously and pointing in my direction.

Later the same day I faced the Captain once more, but this time in his cabin. He told me I had behaved very foolishly and, but for my youth and Mr Darwin's pleading, I would have been flogged most severely. After some thought, he decided my punishment would be less drastic. I was to be confined to the ship for one week and made to scrub the deck from morning till night. I was also put on a diet of ship's biscuits and water. My absence from the ship was never mentioned again and I know it was never reported to the Admiralty in London.

Mr Darwin arranged to stay on at Bahia Blanca before continuing his journey to Buenos Aires. The Captain agreed to his proposal and as I was now forgiven I was allowed to stay too! Before he set out, Mr Darwin decided to undertake some new explorations and ride out over the plains to some distant rocks. This was a dangerous thing to do, as there was a great risk of attack by Indians. However, when he set his mind to do something, there was nothing that could stop him. So it was that we set out to Punta Alta which was, at first sight, a boring place of mud, gravel, sand and flat plain. We spent the day scraping about in the earth and collecting rock samples.

Suddenly, Mr Darwin gave a start of surprise, and called me over to see what he had found. Sticking out of the soft rock was an enormous bone. As we worked feverishly away at the surrounding rock, we uncovered more bones. Even I could sense that they were very old but the thing I did not know was that they all belonged to one skeleton. Mr Darwin was greatly excited.

'It's as big as a rhinoceros, George! But I don't expect you know what that is!'

I shook my head in puzzlement.

'We have discovered a giant,' continued Mr Darwin. 'Truly, George, it is an animal of gigantic size and this skeleton is very, very old. Today the animal is extinct.'

Once again, I gave him a puzzled look. 'You must think me very stupid, sir, but truly I do not know the meaning of that word.'

A smile lit up his face. 'Extinct, George! Died out. Dead – long ago! Don't you see? This is an animal that lived ages ago and there came a time when the very last one perished.

I looked again at the extraordinary collection of bones we had uncovered.

Mr Darwin continued. 'I have come to the conclusion that animals come and animals go! Why, even man might one day disappear from the earth forever!'

That last remark made me look at him sharply.

'Captain FitzRoy would not agree with that, sir. He says that we all come from Adam and Eve and the Garden of Eden. We shall only disappear when it is God's will.'

Mr Darwin smiled gently. 'Unlike Captain FitzRoy, George, I do not know all the answers, but then I am a failed priest. I ask many questions and I seek answers to them, but they do not come to me with ease. I believe the creature whose bones we have just found lived at a time when there were no men on the earth!'

My eyes opened wider. What was he trying to say?

74

'It does not tell us that in the Holy Bible, sir. Truly, you speak strangely. Captain FitzRoy . . .'

'Ah Captain FitzRoy, George! He and I have talked about this matter and we have agreed to disagree! All I seek is truth and if I find it I shall write about it. Perhaps one day I shall put it all down in a book. When your reading improves, as I am sure it will, you will do me the honour of looking at it!'

We stayed some weeks at Bahia Blanca and during that time we saw more of the wildlife of the area. One day Mr Darwin and I had gone down to a river estuary which was a swampy area of mudflats where we could take cover among tall reeds. We peered out over the tidal mudflats and to our astonishment spotted the strangest-looking birds. They were exceedingly tall, and four of them strode over the dried mud on their long legs. They peered around them for fear of attack and their enormous eyes seemed to stick out

from their bald heads. They looked like ostriches! I did not have to be very clever to work out that they could not fly. For one thing, they appeared to be far too heavy and, for another, they had only tiny wings. They pecked at grass and the roots of plants growing on the edge of the estuary. We also saw them searching for fish in little streams on the mudflats. I wanted to get nearer to take a better look but as I crawled towards them they spotted me. Immediately, they ran away in alarm flapping their silly wings to no avail, their long legs carrying them at great speed until they entered a clump of tall reeds. There they disappeared from view, but Mr Darwin was determined to find out what had happened to them.

With the greatest stealth we approached the reed-bed and made our way towards the middle. Imagine my surprise when I parted some reeds with my hands and found myself staring face-to-face at a fiercesome bird! Perhaps it was as surprised as I was since it had been squatting out of sight! The bird hissed horribly at me as I fell backwards in fright. It flapped its wings, and aimed one foot in my direction. Its claws missed me by inches, and I do believe that I was very lucky not to have been severely injured by its kick.

Fortunately for me, the bird raced away through the reeds with the other three in hot pursuit. Mr Darwin pulled me to my feet and although my heart was still pounding with fear, we watched the birds run into the river and swim for a nearby island. When I had got my breath back, Mr Darwin told me that these ostrich-like birds were called rheas.

During the months of September and October we were to find rhea eggs all over the countryside. They were enormous, larger than coconuts, and we found many just on their own amongst stones on the rocky ground. The gauchos told me that eggs laid like these never hatched. One day we were fortunate enough to discover a proper rhea nest. Neither of us really believed what we had discovered. Lying in a large, scraped-out-hollow in the ground were twenty-two gigantic eggs. We counted them three times just to make sure! Later in the day, whilst Mr Darwin spend some time collecting samples of rock, I made another of my little excursions. This time I felt that I was in real luck as I stumbled across a second rhea nest and in it counted no less than twenty-seven eggs! I handled them very carefully and the last one I lifted felt warm to my bare hands. I decided that the rhea parent would not miss one, so I took an egg from the nest. I clambered upon my horse using one hand, while I grasped the egg firmly with the other, and held it close to my chest as I rode away.

There was a sudden scurry of movement from behind a bush and from out of a cloud of dust there raced an enraged, hissing parent. I kicked my horse into action, although it was no less terrified than I was. The furious bird caught up with us and leapt and kicked. Two or three times it nearly knocked me out of the saddle. In my haste to escape, I fear that I dropped and smashed the egg but did not look back as we galloped away from our attacker. A few minutes later I rejoined Mr Darwin and I am ashamed to say that I did not tell him of my adventure, but pretended that my horse and I had enjoyed a good gallop across the plain.

Mr Darwin later told me that he had heard that it is the male rhea that sits on the eggs or, when taking a short rest, sits on guard nearby. As you may imagine, I did not contradict him! He also said that the gauchos had found nests with up to fifty eggs in them! Only when the eggs are laid together do they hatch. He told me that it was believed that four or five female rheas may use a single nest which would explain, of course, the extraordinary number of eggs to be found in one.

We stayed on at Bahia Blanca for some time before I rejoined the Beagle. Mr Darwin continued his journey north to Buenos Aires, taking with him a single gaucho guide. Mr Harris was exceedingly worried by this arrangement, but Mr Darwin, as brave as ever, was prepared to risk his life in the cause of his discoveries. I begged him to let me go with him but he wold not hear of it and, in any case, Captain FitzRoy insisted that I became a crew member once more. So, with tears in my eyes, I bade farewell to my great friend.

He set out on September 8th 1833, and I was not to see him again until December of that year. When he returned to the ship.

I asked Mr Darwin to tell me of the animals he had seen and I confess that I was very envious when he spoke of his discoveries.

'I saw armadillos, George! They are the most curious creatures to observe as they scuttle around with plates of armour over their backs. Unfortunately for them, their meat makes rather a tasty stew and, once stripped of their plating, they are a particular favourite with the gauchos. Near Bahia Blanca, shortly after you departed, I made a trip out to

some coastal sand dunes. My gaucho guide suddenly tumbled out of his saddle and hit the ground. In an instant he was up on his knees, scraping away at the sand. As I joined him, I could see the reason for his activity. A small armadillo had started a burrow to escape him and kicked sand in his face as he crouched to grip the creature. I'm glad to say that it got away and my companion did not find it again!

'On the road to Buenos Aires we spotted an apar, which is another kind of armadillo. A stray dog from a local ranch had joined up with us during this part of the journey. In fact, it was he who first discovered the apar and rushed at it in great excitement. As soon as the apar saw the attack coming it rolled up in a tight ball and the poor dog was quite unable to bite it. The wretched creature was no doubt very hungry, but he was out of luck as the apar refused to unroll for him!'

Mr Darwin went on to tell me of another adventure which took place on the River Paraná, one of the great rivers leading down to the Rio de la Plata.

'The Paraná is full of islands,' he told me. 'They lie low just above the water and are made from the mud and sand washed down river all year. At times of flood, some islands disappear altogether and are never seen again. It is extremely dangerous to explore these islands even when the river is not in flood. They abound with willow trees held together by thick creepers and, to be frank, it is almost impossible to push you way in. One evening, I foolishly went off by myself to discover the innermost secrets of one large island. Soon after I got onto the island I spotted freshly made tracks of a wild animal. I could see that it had broad, padded feet but I was not sure what it could be. Then I spotted a nearby tree whose bark, low down on one side, was worked smooth. Either side of this patch I saw distinct claw marks. Long scratches extended down the trunk and it was clear to me that the marks had been made recently.

Mr Darwin paused for a moment and I took the opportunity to press him to tell me more.

'What kind of animal had made these marks, sir?'

'To be truthful, I asked myself the very same question, George, and as soon as I had the answer I beat a hasty retreat. They were the claw marks of the jaguar, which is a strong and powerful member of the cat family. I had the horrible feeling that I was being watched by terrible yellow eyes from somewhere deep in the thicket ahead of me. Of course, I stood no chance of seeing the beast as its spots give it perfect camouflage and it is able to slink low to the ground before making its deadly attack. I was most relieved to get back to the safety of my party.'

81

This was the first time I had heard Mr Darwin admit to being afraid.

'Surely, sir, it would not attack a man?' I asked him.

'To be sure it most certainly would, George!' he replied 'I met a man who had been attacked whilst sleeping on the open deck of his boat, which was moored to the riverbank. He had been badly savaged by a jaguar and one of his arms has never recovered and is useless. Woodcutters set up camps along the riverbanks and I heard tales of how many had been killed. Do you know, George, I even heard tell of a large jaguar that entered a village church? It lay in wait for its next victims, who were two priests. A third priest was lucky to escape with his life!'

Mr Darwin looked very grave as he finished his tale.

'I have listened to a jaguar roaring at night in nearby jungle,' he went on. 'I and my companions sat in terror waiting for the attack which, I am glad to say, never came. That deep-throated roar sends shivers up the spines of the bravest men and I do not count myself amongst them. I was petrified!'

That made me think a while and I did not regret the fact that I had been forced to return to the Beagle, and had missed this part of Mr Darwin's adventures.

Mr Darwin spent much time telling me of his adventures on land. He descibed a flat, dry plain, full of low bushes, each one bristling and prickling with thorns.

'At night, George, the plain blazes with the lights of fires as far as the eye can see. The army from Buenos Aires, under the command of General Rosas, is determined to hunt down every Indian. The soldiers clear the land by burning it as they go and the fires confuse the Indians. As the thorn bushes are destroyed, ranchers move onto the land to set up their farms. One day, grass plains will stretch across the horizon and enormous herds of beef cattle will graze in this country. The gauchos will find much work to do and there will be no Indians or wild animals to interfere with them. The cattle ranchers will change the face of the countryside forever.'

Mountains and earthquakes

You will remember our adventures of Tierra del Feugo, the Land of Fire, which was the home of Jemmy Button and his friends. In June 1834 we bade farewell forever to this forbidding land and began a journey north hugging the coast of a new country. This was Chile which, if you look it up in an atlas, you will find stretches for much of the length of the west coast of South America. We surveyed any number of

small islands and channels which lie off the shores of the southern part of the country. As we sailed away from the storms and biting winds of Cape Horn our spirits revived. We had at last reached the Pacific Ocean, the world's largest sea. Great sailors and navigators in the past had risked life and limb to find a way to the Pacific and its spice islands. Now we followed in their wake.

Late in July 1834 the Beagle anchored in the bay of Valparaiso, a town built, so it seemed, out of steep, narrow valleys running down to the sea. We had arrived at night and next morning I was awakened by the sounds of the town as the sun climbed over the hilltops. The hot rays of the sun shone brightly from a cloudless sky and from our anchorage I could make out straggling lines of tiny, white-washed dwellings with brightly tiled red roofs. How I longed to be on land!

Mr Darwin came up from below and stood beside me on the deck. He peered into the distance far beyond the town and the surrounding hills.

'Do you see mountains, George? Away to the north-east lie the Andes, which dwarf these little "molehills" in front of us. In the Andes are to be found some of the world's highest mountains.'

Mr Darwin arranged to meet an old schoolfriend who had made his home in Valparaiso. Some days later he set out on horseback and told me later of his discoveries.

'We rode north, George, along the coast and then struck inland to the foothills of the Andes which, being summer, we were able to explore. In winter they are cut off by the snow. My friend had told me of ancient seashells lying in rocks at some distance above sea level.'

Mr Darwin eagerly pulled a shell from his pocket and showed it to me.

85

'I found this little shell in the mountains thirteen hundred feet above sea level. Do you not think that is remarkable.?'

Indeed, I did think it was most strange and, if truth be told, I could not for the life of me understand how seashells could be found half way up a mountain!

'The land in these parts has risen, George. Great forces below the surface of the earth have, over a long period of time, caused the land to twist and buckle. It rose out of the sea. Locked away in the rock was this small shell and millions like it.'

I blinked at Mr Darwin with some disbelief.

'But sir, how can land move? It lookes solid enough to me. I have seen the sea go up and down, that's for sure, but rock is surely too hard to be pushed so high? In any case, sir, what causes the pushing – not the wind I imagine?'

Mr Darwin nodded in agreement with me.

'I believe that if we could bore a hole down through the rock, deep, deep down, George, we should undertake the most exciting journey of all. The voyage of the Beagle would be dull compared to that. It is thought that in some parts of the world, there are enormous forces and heat melting minerals and rocks below the earth. It is as though there is a fiery furnace beneath our feet where forces build up and cause all sorts of changes above. I am talking of changes that take place so slowly that you would need to live perhaps millions of years to notice them. That is something which none of us can expect to do, not even Captain FitzRoy!'

I felt very unsure of what Mr Darwin was telling me.

'The Captain tells me that the world was created in seven days, Mr Darwin. God made light, the sea and the land so he must have made the mountains at the same time!' I explained.

Mr Darwin smiled and shook his head slightly.

'It is also said that God moves in a mysterious way. Will the Captain explain how seashells came to be locked up in mountain rocks?'

'I cannot say, Mr Darwin. You tell me one thing and the Captain another. How ever shall I find out the truth?'

Mr Darwin put his hand on my shoulder and spoke gently.

'The truth, George, is something you must find out for yourself. It is like a voyage of discovery and you will meet many adventures on the way. Listen to people's opinions but in the end it must be for you to determine truth as you find it.'

How I wished to accompany Mr Darwin on all his adventures and share his thoughts. Unfortunately, my job was to stay with the ship and attend to the needs of the Captain and his officers.

Mr Darwin continued his explorations but in the course of time I would hear about them in great detail. For one thing he was a very busy writer and always took the trouble to make notes in a little book, even at the tops of mountains or during a storm at sea. It was some time later that I heard about his exploration of the Andes.

'My first real mountain was the Campana, which we would call the Bell mountain. Stunted bushes grew upon the northern slope whilst on the southern slope was a bamboo forest and even a few palm trees. Our horses had the greatest difficulty in keeping their feet on the rugged paths. We made camp by a spring and looked back over the bay of Valparaiso where I could make out the masts of what seemed to be toy ships. That night, as the sun set behind the mountains, I stood in wonder at the beauty and majesty of nature. Beyond us rose the snow-covered tops of the Andes glinting deep red in the evening sky.

'Next day, we ascended the summit and gazed across a range of mountains stretching into the distance. We could make out the snow line and just now and again the high cone of a volcano. Because of the fires and stresses in the earth below, certain metals have been caused to melt and run into bands in the rocks. Later they cooled and became solid metal, to be mined. Our mountain was like a rabbit warren of holes tunnelled in the search for gold. The poor Chileans in the mines have a very bad time and work with almost no machinery. I have even seen them carrying water out of the mines in leather bags because they have no pumps to do the job.'

I myself saw some of these half-starved miners in the town and felt dreadfully sorry for them.

Soon, however, we set sail in the Beagle to carry on our map work for the Navy, leaving Mr Darwin to continue his work. We were not to know that he became ill at the end of September, and for a whole month was confined to bed in the house of his friend. When we met up with him later in the year he seemed thinner and slightly older.

We spent the first few weeks of 1835 surveying the southern coast of Chile, and then we set sail for the port of Valdivia. When we arrived, Mr Darwin rode up into the hills to look for new plants and animals. A small party from the Beagle went ashore to collect fresh water and provisions. We had made our way along the main street of the town with its small wooden houses, when suddenly I felt the ground beneath my feet begin to tremble. Captain FitzRoy quickly ordered us away from the houses which began to rattle and shake. One tilted over at an angle as a mother ran out of it, carrying a baby in her arms. People began to scream in panic as the ground heaved and swelled. We were knocked over and lay on the ground in fear. Dogs howled and children cried as their mothers prayed to their Maker. Truly, I thought it to be the end of the world and imagined that I should be swallowed in the furnace of fire beneath. Suddenly it was over. The houses, some of them badly cracked, returned to their normal positions. Windows and doors hung open on their remaining hinges. Quietness reigned as some of the horror-struck townsfolk struggled to their feet. Others remained on their knees to praise God for their deliverance.

Later in the day Mr Darwin returned from the forest and told us how he had fared during the earthquake. He had not suffered so badly.

'It was similar to walking the deck in a high sea,' he explained. 'I felt giddy and had the horrible feeling that I was standing on thin ice which would crack at any time. The creatures of the forest remained quiet and in some mysterious way I felt that they knew what was coming.'

Only a few weeks later, in March, we landed at Talcahuano, a town of some size. We were deeply shocked to see only the remains of what had once been a prosperous port. Another earthquake had shaken the houses so badly that they had tumbled upon one another. People trod like ghosts through the jumble of stones and timbers, searching for their possessions, and thieves lurked amongst the ruins.

Nearly one hundred people had been killed and if the quake had taken place at night it might have claimed hundreds more.

Some days later, upon a nearby island, Mr Darwin met a man who had had an interesting experience. He was out riding when he and his horse were thrown to the ground which heaved beneath them. In terror, he watched as a herd of cows grazing on a nearby hillside was rolled into the ocean. A wave started far out to sea and increased to gigantic size as it approached the shore. Panic spread to the inhabitants of the nearby coast as the wave swept towards them. It rushed into the bay and tore into their houses and a small fort, where a heavy cannon and its carriage were washed away. A sailing ship was carried two hundred yards inland by the water.

Now I began to understand the words of Mr Darwin when he told me of the power of the earth below, which can twist and change the surface. It made me respect the forces of nature both on land and at sea. I felt small and helpless when I thought of all the things I had seen. Yet nature has its delights, too, and I was soon to discover more of these.

Galapagos, giant tortoises and sea dragons

On September 7th 1835 the Beagle sailed away from South America and headed north-west across the Pacific Ocean. Captain FitzRoy had been ordered to survey a group of small islands lying on the Equator. Thus we had before us a sea journey of some five hundred miles. On board the ship Mr Darwin was always busy writing letters and making notes. He asked me to help him with the many plants he had collected on the mainland; it seemed that he had so much stuff that he could grow his own jungle. Captain FitzRoy was not overpleased to find his cabin filled with half the wildlife of South America. There were skins of reptiles and birds, shells and bones – all manner of things. I could not imagine that yet any more creatures were to be found. Mr Darwin, as you may imagine, looked forward to our next adventure.

I asked him the name of the islands to which we were bound.

'Galapagos, so I am told,' he said, 'the Galapagos Islands. The Captain tells me they are volcanic. We have known storms on this voyage, revolutions and earthquakes and now we may discover the excitements of a volcano! Sparks and dust filling the sky as a mountain rises from the sea! Streams of molten lava cascading down the sides of the volcano, spitting and sliding into the ocean!

I was horrified at such a picture and told Mr Darwin so. It seemed to me that I had escaped death enough times already without putting my life further at risk. I had seen enough danger to last me a lifetime and knew that life was precious. During our journey I had been taught to read and write and I had plans to see more of the world and its strange animals and plants. For me, the Galapagos Islands might mean an end to my ambitions and I did not look forward to our landing there.

'Land ahoy!' A shout went up from the look-out perched high in the rigging. We scrambled to the side of the ship and within minutes black, forbidding tops of volcanoes came into view. As we sailed closer I could make out the uninviting, rocky coastline of black lava. We landed on Chatham Island where the lava shore sloped down to the ocean from high volcanic hills. Great cracks, wide enough for a man to fall down, stretched across this bleak landscape and a little way up we saw strunted trees struggling to survive in the simmering heat of the noonday sun. To me, it was the most horrible of all the places we had visited.

Farther inland we discoverd a forest of giant cactuses, each plant bristling with prickles and defying our progress. I had fallen and grazed my knees several times on the rough, hard lava and was exhausted. Ahead of us was a rounded mound upon which I clambered and sat down. Suddenly the mound moved and I swayed, clinging onto its smooth face. I was being carried away and could do nothing to save myself! The mound hissed and lurched. Mr Darwin and the two sailors accompanying him were helpless with laughter. I was too terrified to ask why and in a moment I found myself sliding to the ground where I lay sprawled and winded. The mound put out its head and gave out another frightful hiss. It was alive! A scaly head with hard, black eyes swung out upon a long leathery neck.

'Run George!' cried Mr Darwin. 'Run before it

devours you boy! It moves like lightning!' he roared with laughter.

The sailors screamed at this poor joke and I felt exceedingly foolish. The creature, for that is what it was, clumped slowly away on four thick legs covered in scales. Enormous claws protruded from each of its feet.

'You've been taken for a ride, George!' laughed Mr Darwin. 'The giant tortoise of the Galapagos! Only you could sit down on one by accident!'

I admitted my foolish error and smiled sheepishly. To be truthful, in the days we spent on the islands I grew to like the great tortoises. I was saddened to learn that they were hunted for their meat and killed in their hundreds.

It was our duty to survey all the islands of the Galapagos and on one, named Albemarle, we saw smoke rising from one of the volcanic craters. On the coast we came across huge black lizards with long tails, basking in the sun, or clinging to the rocks while the waves dashed over them. They looked like dragons coming out of the sea. Up in the hills we discovered yellowish-brown lizards which, on our approach, scrambled into their burrows. I have never seen such ugly, lazy creatures before or since. They seemed extremely stupid as they crawled away from us dragging their bellies and tails over the rock and stopping every now and then for a doze in the warm sun.

Mr Darwin had gone to meet the vice-governor of the Galapagos Islands and on his return I could see that he had been given something to think about.

'It is all very puzzling,' he explained to me, one day, as we explored a forest of bamboos. 'The vice-governor tells me that the tortoises are different on each of these islands! He can tell which island he is on simply by looking at the sort of tortoise living there. Yet these islands are very similar to each other. They are all volcanic and lie just about on the Equator quite close to each other. So why should the tortoises be different?'

As ever, I had no answer for him.

'And think of the mocking-thrushes, George. We have spotted them flying about. There is one kind on Charles Island, another on Albemarle and there is a third type to be found on James and Chatham Islands. I am also puzzled by the variety of finches. Once again I have noticed that this bird is different on the the different islands.'

As I have mentioned before, I knew Mr Darwin to

be a clever man and only rarely did I find him at a loss for an answer. Suddenly, I began to understand the problem.

'You mean, sir, that these Galapagos Islands are new? They were not created at the beginning of the world but long, long after?

'Yes, George, I do! The sea was here before the islands. They rose out of the ocean in their volcanic way.'

I tried to get things clearer in my mind.

'First, sir, there was the sea?'

'Correct!' he said.

'Then came the islands?'

'Precisely,' he agreed.

'And then, once the lava cooled down on the islands, came the plants and the animals?' I suggested.

'Yes,' he agreed. 'But how? How did they arrive?'

Once again I had no answer.

'Do you remember, George, early in the voyage, that dust cloud we met far out to sea?' he asked me. 'Amongst the dust we found tiny plant spores.'

'You said, sir, that the spores had been blown from land hundreds of miles away. Africa, I believe.'

'Yes George! But now we are hundreds of miles off South America. I believe that the wind carried spores and seeds to these islands from the mainland. Some would land upon the thin soil made from the volcanic rock and they would grow. Very slowly, and it would take a long time, vegetation would gain a foothold upon these islands.'

This made a certain amount of sense to me but there was one question which I found more puzzling than ever.

'I can see how plant life might find its way here sir,

but that does not explain how the animals came to the islands.'

'That is very nearly the most important question of all,' he told me. 'Can you imagine how birds might get here?'

That was an easy one!'

'Why, they would fly, sir!' I replied.

'Yes, of course they would!' he laughed. 'But there would have to be a reason for some of them to fly out to sea. Think of the mocking-thrush and the tiny finch. They are not sea birds! I believe that some may have been blown here by accident. They may have been caught in a gale and swept miles out to sea. A few lucky survivors might just have struggled this far!'

'But that does not explain the lizards and tortoises and other land animals, Mr Darwin. How did they get here?' I asked him. He shook his head.

'I can only suggest that they may have been carried here by the sea currents,' he explained. 'You remember the earthquakes and how we saw houses and trees thrown to the ground? Some trees would be swept out to sea, perhaps caught and held together by their branches. Over a long period of time just a few might have been washed up on the island shores. It is possible that animals might have been caught up amongst them!'

'You mean like life-rafts on a boat, sir? The animals would be stranded on the floating vegetation as it was carried away from the mainland?' I asked him.

'I do, George! I mean just that. It is a possibility. How else could land animals reach here otherwise? But there is still the greatest question of all to be answered,' he told me.

By now I thought that there could be no more questions to answer.

'Think George, think!' he exclaimed, growing excited. 'Different tortoises on different islands. Different finches on different islands. Do you really think that each island received a different sort of tortoise from the tree rafts? No! It was the same kind of tortoise. And it was the same kind of finch that was blown here. They started off the same on all the islands.' His voice rose in excitement. 'Now, years and years later, they are different!

I stared at him in astonishment and begged him to speak lower lest the sailors should hear.

'That can't be, sir!' I whispered. 'Captain FitzRoy would tell you that. You are telling me that animals change! But that just can't be! It's impossible.'

Mr Darwin clasped his forehead in his hand. He was shaking as he spoke. 'I don't know, George! I just don't know! It is not a new idea. Other people have thought that living things change too. But here on Galapagos we have the evidence! I am simply not sure of myself and need time to think. Tomorrow we leave the islands. I shall never have another chance to return. There is something here which tells me that we have made a very great discovery!'

Poor Mr Darwin! He had got himself into a terrible state and I had to help him back to the boat. Next day we sailed and bade farewell to those bleak, black islands with their strange animals.

Through paradise to home

Now began a new adventure. We sailed across the Pacific Ocean, calling in at the most exotic islands, with so many things to see. I secretly noted a slight change in Mr Darwin. It came about very slowly but I, who knew him well, felt that he had become a deeper person and more serious. He brooded in his cabin for hours on end whilst at other times he paced about on the deck. The sailors had got into the habit of calling him 'Philosopher' on account of his thinking and I knew, too that the Captain and Mr Darwin became involved in rows. Late in the year, only a few days before Christmas, we sighted New Zealand and made our landing. In the New Year, 1836, we called in at Sydney, Australia, but in neither country did we stay very long. I continued to worry on Mr Darwin's behalf and hoped that our journey across the Indian Ocean to the Keeling Islands would revive his flagging spirits.

On April 1st we obtained our first view of Keeling Island itself, composed entirely of coral. The Beagle passed carefully along a shallow channel between jagged outcrops of coral rock. In this way we passed into the calm waters of a lagoon and rested at anchor. Behind us lay a line of white breakers, which pounded upon the coral, and in the azure blue sky above a puff of cloud drifted out to sea. Yet as we peered over the side of the ship the water appeared emerald green above the whitest sand. On land we made out the dark tops of coconut trees swaying gently in the breeze. To me, this was paradise, and I was cheered to find Mr Darwin returned more to his old self.

Next morning, we set foot on Direction Island. The lagoon shore upon which we landed was chalky and extremely hot, though here and there we found a patch of sand. I was much surprised to find that the island was extremely narrow and no sooner had we entered a plantation of coconut trees than we were out the other side. Here, the sound of the surf reached our ears as the great rolling waves broke and dashed upon the coral out to sea. It amazed me that trees could grow in such a place. On the coral shores small hermit crabs scurried around and, overhead, resting in the trees, we spotted frigate birds and gannets. Mr Darwin was enchanted. He had spotted a small snow-white tern.

'There George, above your head! Don't move, it is only just above you. See how it hovers! Why it is like a fairy spirit! Have you ever seen a creature so magical?' he asked.

We met some of the islanders as we explored each new coral paradise. Mr Darwin took a special interest in the coral and lost no chance of studying it. He made many notes and drawings in his notebook. The islanders were poor folk, yet they seemed fit enough on their diet of fish, turtles and coconuts. We found them pleasant and generous and Mr Darwin seemed much charmed by them.

One day, we had set out in a small party to explore a channel which wound its way between outcrops of coral. Ahead of us we heard a shout and spotted two canoes in the lagoon. In the bow of one stood a man peering excitedly into the water. His companions paddled furiously and he swayed this way and that to keep his balance. We watched, fascinated, as he dived into the water and thrashed about yelling and laughing. He was in no trouble but we rowed

towards him. In a moment it became clear to us what he was doing. He was a fisherman and had jumped onto the back of a sea turtle which had been forced to break the surface to breathe air. The man hung on to it as it attempted to escape, his fingers gripping firmly onto the shell around its neck. Of course, we had to follow to find out the fate of the turtle, which, after a few minutes, slowed down and became exhausted. It could offer no more resistance and was roped to the side of the canoe. Turtle meat is quite delicious when roasted over a charcoal fire.

I made friends with the fishermen and not many days later was allowed to paddle a small canoe all on my own across the lagoon. There was a tiny coral island which had taken my interest and I landed upon it and made off to explore. Pushing my way amongst the coconut trees I found a shady spot where I could sit and dream. The sea breeze rustled the green, pointed fronds over my head and in the distance the surf pounded upon the coral. I turned over, lay on my back and gazed out to sea.

All of a sudden, there was a tapping sound. I raised my head and listened intently. There it was again! Distinctly I heard a sound of short repeated knockings. I looked slowly round and came face to face with a monstrous creature! An enormous crab waved a gigantic and terrifying claw in my direction. It was little more than arm's length from me and it lay, half-hidden, beneath the root of a tree. To my astonishment, it drove its claw into a coconut which lay on the ground. Immediately, I realised that I was not to be attacked. The brown fibres of the coconut covering lay shredded upon the sand and the crab repeatedly hammered its pincer at the 'eye', or weak spot, of the nut. A hole was made and I watched the crab turn round in a clumsy fashion and use its small pincers to work out the thick white flesh.

I did not fear the crab any more. When I saw Mr Darwin again on my return to the Beagle he was most interested to learn about it. He told me that he had heard that certain of these crabs actually climbed trees to capture the nuts! He had not seen it for himself but was hoping that he might get the chance. Mr Darwin also spoke of a giant crab that had been kept alive in a tin biscuit-box. Although wire had been used to secure the lid, the animal soon escaped. It made a pretty mess of the tin in doing so!

Now, I near the end of my tale. The Beagle continued her voyage across the Indian Ocean. We sailed past Madagascar and round the southern tip of Africa and crossed the South Atlantic Ocean. The Trade Winds sped us across the seas towards Brazil and we called in at Bahia where, four and a half years earlier we had lain at anchor.

During the voyage I had grown from a boy to a young man. We had sailed round the world and here, five thousand miles from home, we now prepared for our last voyage. Our weary crew, officers and men, were finally going home. Mr Darwin probably looked forward to his home-coming more than most.

'To England, George! To glorious England! You cannot imagine how much I long for her green fields and woodlands. We have seen the world; mountains two or three miles high; tropical islands and the Brazilian jungle, yet to me England is ten times more lovely. I do not wish to travel again. I intend to lead a peaceful life and take a house in the country. There I shall be content!'

Thus it was that we left Brazil in August and anchored off Falmouth in Cornwall on October 2nd

1836. I was very sad to say goodbye to my friend Mr Darwin. We had seen many things together, but now our adventure had come to an end. I joined another ship only a few weeks later and have spent the rest of my life at sea as humble George Carter, Able Seaman.

It was foolish of me to lose touch with Mr Darwin for I had promised to practise my writing and send him letters from ports across the world. Yet I never forgot him in my thoughts and during many nights at sea I have dreamt of the days of our great adventure. There is a sad tale to tell, too, as I learnt many years later that Captain FitzRoy had become ill and had taken his own life.

So here ends my story. Yet perhaps it is not quite over for only recently did I purchase a book in a shop in Plymouth. The book was called 'The Origin of Species' and my attention was drawn to it by the name of the author on its cover. His name was Darwin. The bookseller informed me that 'this Darwin fellow has created a dreadful rumpus. Why! He has turned the whole world upside down and has made enemies in high circles.'

I have the book with me now on my new ship and shall read it during our voyage. It seems impossible to me that the gentle, mild-mannered Mr Darwin could make enemies. I wonder too, what the man meant by 'high circles'. However I intend to find out for it appears that my friend Mr Darwin has become a very famous person!

Why I wrote this book

This book is an adventure story based closely on the diaries of Darwin's exploits on his famous round-the-world voyage. The young Charles Darwin was a likeable, bold person with a great thirst for travel and new experiences. Later in his life he suffered an illness which sapped much of his physical energy. It was during these long years that his mind turned to his scientific theory of evolution by natural selection.

The young Charles Darwin was greatly liked by professors of Geology and Botany at Cambridge University although he was not supposed to be studying these subjects! They appreciated his brilliant, enquiring mind. When the opportunity came for a ship's botanist to travel with the Royal Naval Frigate HMS *Beagle*, Darwin's name was put forward. He soon made friends with the officers and crew and four people travelling on the ship who were returning to their homes in Patagonia at the southern tip of South America.

Darwin was fearless and was prepared to run the risk of night attacks by wild jungle animals in Brazil or local people whose very existence was threatened by the European colonists. It is likely that the illness which Charles Darwin suffered from in later life was picked up during the last few months of his exploits along the Pacific coast of South America.

Peter ward